Geographical Data Imperfection 2

Geographical Data Imperfection 2

Use Cases

Edited by

François Pinet
Mireille Batton-Hubert
Eric Desjardin

WILEY

First published 2023 in Great Britain and the United States by ISTE Ltd and John Wiley & Sons, Inc.

ISTE Ltd
27-37 St George's Road
London SW19 4EU
UK

www.iste.co.uk

John Wiley & Sons, Inc.
111 River Street
Hoboken, NJ 07030
USA

www.wiley.com

Library of Congress Control Number: 2023944988

British Library Cataloguing-in-Publication Data
A CIP record for this book is available from the British Library
ISBN 978-1-78630-298-4

Contents

Chapter 4. The Representation of Uncertainty Applied to Natural Risk Management

Jean-François GIRRES

Chapter 5. Incorporating Uncertainty Into Victim Location Processes in the Mountains: A Methodological, Software and Cognitive Approach

Matthieu VIRY, Mattia BUNEL, Marlène VILLANOVA, Ana-Maria
OLTEANU-RAIMOND, Cécile DUCHÊNE and Paule-Annick DAVOINE

**Chapter 6. Uncertainties Related to Real Estate
Price Estimation Scales**   127
Didier JOSSELIN, Delphine BLANKE, Mathieu COULON, Guilhem BOULAY,
Laure CASANOVA ENAULT, Antoine PERIS, Pierre LE BRUN and
Thibault LECOURT

Chapter 7. Representing Urban Space for the Visually Impaired. 165
Lisa DENIS, Jérémy KALSRON and Jean-Marie FAVREAU

Preface

Geographic data often contain imperfections that are related to a lack of precision, errors, incomplete data, etc. If these imperfections are not identified, taken into account and controlled when using these data, then risks of errors can appear and lead to important consequences with unforeseeable effects, especially in a decision-making context. It is then necessary to characterize and model this imperfection, and then to take it into account throughout the processing.

In the previous volume, we presented different approaches to define, represent and deal with the imperfection of geographic data. In this volume, we present several concrete applications in various domains: agriculture, natural disaster management, mountain risks, land management and assistance to visually impaired people.

The book is organized as follows. Chapter 1 aims at modeling the uncertainty of agricultural inputs on plots using fuzzy subsets. One of the objectives is to estimate the possible quantities of products during agricultural treatment coverage over time. Chapter 2 analyzes the evolution of land use from the agricultural parcel register. The methods presented take into account the imperfect nature of the spatial objects and extract the different spatiotemporal relationships existing between the objects. Chapter 3 shows how it is possible to voluntarily integrate uncertainty in data in order to guarantee the confidentiality of personal information, while allowing an exploitation of aggregated data. The application concerns agricultural areas. Chapter 4 shows how uncertainty is taken into account in the delimitation of danger areas associated with natural hazards, and how it is represented in cartographic documents. Chapter 5 proposes the elaboration of a logical reasoning model allowing us to go from descriptions of relative location to the construction of possible geolocalized zones. The simultaneous consideration of verbatim and their transcription by a spatial analysis manipulating imprecision and uncertainty is developed in the context of victim location in the mountains. Chapter 6 is devoted to the uncertainty on the estimation of real estate prices for a geographical area. It considers, in particular, the uncertainty related to the "statistical-spatial" distribution of prices by evaluating the effect of spatial support on real estate price estimates for different territorial grids. Chapter 7 is devoted to the role of landmarks in the construction of urban routes for visually impaired people. The aim is to integrate the uncertainty concerning both the permanence and the reliability of a geographic object and its modeling in an adapted ontology and finally to propose a method of integration in the multimodal map.

This book is the result of the collective work of the prospective action *Incertitude épistémique : des données aux modèles en géomatique* (Epistemic Uncertainty: From Data to Models in Geomatics) of the CNRS MAGIS Research Group. We would like to thank all of the members of the action for their work and reflections that led to this book, and we wish readers a pleasant reading.

François PINET, Mireille BATTON-HUBERT and Eric DESJARDIN
September 2023

Implementation and Computation of Fuzzy Geographic Objects in Agriculture

1.1. Fuzzy geographic objects

A spatial object is an object with a geographical extension. Like any object, it has properties and connections with other objects, whether they are spatial or not. Furthermore, some more or less complex processes can occur on this object. Often, the processes also have a spatial dimension and occur on the geographical extension. This exact vision of the objects requires that the extension area (the polygon in 2D) of the element is known in order to be positioned on a reference ellipsoid (mathematical model of the Earth) and geolocated. However, there are many cases where the limits of this extension are imprecise (poorly known limits) or even unclear when it is a question, for example, of the probable membership of a point or a geolocated surface to an area. Some imperfections can then be modeled in a fuzzy spatial object. This type of representation makes it possible to identify and manipulate objects with extension zones affected by imperfections. The model proposed in Figure 1.1 shows a fuzzy object composed of a core (the darkest central part) and uncertain parts that appear as concentric zones. The core is the certain part of the object, therefore having a membership degree to the observed process equal to 1. Each concentric zone is associated with a membership degree <1, thus modeling the uncertainty of the phenomenon. These are α-cuts.

Chapter written by Mireille BATTON-HUBERT, François PINET and André MIRALLES.

Figure 1.1. *A representation of a fuzzy geographic object. For a color version of this figure, see www.iste.co.uk/pinet/geographic2.zip*

Let us look at an example from agriculture. Crops are subject to the pressure of bio-aggressors (weeds, diseases, pests, etc.). To limit production losses, farmers use treatment products such as herbicides, insecticides or fungicides with a sprayer. Often, pests are not distributed homogeneously in the field. They are spatially concentrated in "patches" that grow in size as the infestation progresses. Faced with this situation, the farmer has two strategies: either he applies a product in total coverage on the crop or he treats only the patches. This second strategy, which is part of precision agriculture, requires greater technical skills, but above all it requires a prior map of the patches, a sprayer equipped with a geo-localization system and a control of the application to its position. To simplify the presentation of our examples, we will hereafter concentrate only on the first strategy, that is, applications in total coverage, and in cases of arable crops (wheat, rape, corn, etc.). In this context, the operational goal is to spread the treatment products as homogeneously as possible over the plot in order to avoid concentration peaks in certain areas.

To carry out the application, the product is fragmented into droplets (spraying) by nozzles in order to treat the entire plot. To do this, the agricultural machine must make several swaths spaced by the width of the spray boom. As the nozzles have an angular sector (110° for most sprayers), the swaths at the periphery of the agricultural plot often have an uncertain extension (α-cuts), as shown in Figure 1.1. The same is true at the ends of the swaths because the opening or closing of the spray is not instantaneous. If they are parallel and accurately spaced, the swath interfaces receive similar amounts of active ingredient as the rest of the swath. If this is not the case, if the geometric shape of the plot deviates too much from that of a rectangle, if there are obstacles inside the plot, or if the booms swing, this will result in local under- or overdosing. In addition, if applications are made in windy conditions, the droplets may drift significantly, causing a very significant increase in uncertain spread. The problem of local variations of dosage within the spray core are integrated in the quantity of product used approximated by a fuzzy quantity; we focus on modeling the extension around the global treatment area first and then on the associated possible quantity.

In full coverage applications, the nozzle output must be constant to spread the active ingredient evenly. This quantity can be expressed in ng/m². The formula for calculating the volume per acre of spray mixture applied as a function of nozzle output is as follows:

$$V = \frac{600\,n}{L.Vit}Q_{\text{nozzle}} = kQ_{\text{nozzle}}$$

where:

– V is the spray volume per acre to be applied (L/ha);

– n is the number of nozzles on the boom;

– L is the width of the boom (m);

– Vit is the speed of the device (km/h) during processing;

– Q_{nozzle} is the flow rate of a spray nozzle (L/min).

This formula makes it possible to note that, for fixed working conditions (materialized by the coefficient k), the volume per acre spread is directly proportional to the flow rates of the nozzles.

In practice, the entire spray rarely reaches the target. Indeed, at the beginning of the season, the crops only have a few leaves; only a small part of the spraying volume reaches the crop, and the rest goes to the ground. This translates mathematically into the following relationships:

$$V = V_{crop} + V_{soil} \Rightarrow \begin{cases} V_{crop} < V & \Rightarrow \quad \dfrac{V_{crop}}{V} < 1 \\ \\ V_{soil} < V & \Rightarrow \quad \dfrac{V_{soil}}{V} < 1 \end{cases}$$

As the growing season progresses, the leaf mass increases and intercepts more and more of the spray. Correspondingly, the soil receives less and less product. The same relationships can be established for the active ingredient since it is, by dilution, directly proportional to the spray volume per hectare.

The volumes per hectare on the crop (V_{crop}) or on the soil (V_{soil}) and the deposition of active ingredients on the plant (D_{crop}) or on the soil (D_{soil}) can be represented by fuzzy numbers. As these four numbers have relations of proportionality or complementarity, we will only be interested in the continuation in the deposit of active ingredient on the crop (D_{crop})[1]. In practice, when the crop has a very dense leaf mass (e.g. maize), this number can take the value of 1, in the dense zone of the crop, that is, all of the active ingredient from the nozzle is intercepted by the plant and does not reach the soil.

The vision presented here is still a simplified description of the problem. Indeed, other factors can be added, such as the fact that, for treatments during hot periods, part of the deposited products can also evaporate or that, for treatments followed by an unexpected rain, the products are washed off and will run off the ground. These influences make it more difficult to determine the fuzzy spatial object.

In summary, the treatment of an agricultural plot can be represented by a fuzzy spatial object composed of a central part, the core, where the applied dose corresponds to the recommendations of use and of an uncertain spatial extension which receives a lower dose. As the dose received by the crop is a fuzzy number, this leads to the study of the combination of a fuzzy spatial object and a fuzzy number.

---

1 In insecticide and fungicide treatment, the target is the crop, whereas in weed control, the target is the weeds that compete with the crop and colonize the soil. In the first case, we are more interested in the numbers V_{crop} and D_{crop}, while in the second case it is the numbers V_{soil} and D_{soil} that should be studied.

1.2. Evaluation of the deposit on crops: formalizing fuzzy data

The issue of treatment of an agricultural plot shows that the knowledge on the area boundaries is sometimes partial or difficult to estimate, and that the information on the dose of active ingredient received by the crop may also be subject to imprecision and uncertainty. To deal with these factors, we can go beyond the use of the classical operators of spatial analysis, which are the calculation of area (m^2) and mass per unit area (ng/m^2), for the calculation of the total dose of active ingredient applied or the dose of active ingredient per unit area (m^2). More generally, the scalar magnitudes of the spatial object and its attribute properties (which can be manipulated in vector and raster modes) need to be reconsidered. Moreover, the associated semantic model must evolve.

The aim is then to formalize the uncertainty according to the knowledge of the context: we try to estimate the active ingredient dose at a geo-localized point X_p or a geographically limited area X_s, according to its membership to one or several treatment zones of agricultural plots.

Several problems related to the available information can be postulated and then formalized:

– The constraints related to the mechanical treatment device sometimes make the quantity of active ingredient applied to the crop an imprecise quantity and it could thus be represented by a fuzzy number. It is then necessary to evaluate the reliability of the total quantity associated with the treatment area. The formalization and implementation of the spatial tools required for this question form the framework and content of this chapter.

– Boundary information for the treated area is sometimes unclear. The treated area of the plot may be a fuzzy spatial object. The treatment depends on the presence or absence of product on the plants. These two problems are complementary and require considering the formalism of uncertainty and imprecision handled in the case of these so-called fuzzy spatial objects and associated quantities, according to the models presented in (Batton-Hubert et al. 2019). Furthermore, it is incumbent to distinguish the formalisms of uncertainty associated with the description of the objects and quantities handled that are required for the construction of new fuzzy quantities.

First of all, we will briefly recall the concepts and formalisms necessary for the representation of these magnitudes and fuzzy geographical objects, and then we will provide the elementary operators necessary for the processing of these objects within the framework of agricultural processing of parcels. The second part will be devoted to the construction of geographical semantic objects and their implementation in an adapted spatial database. Finally, the last part introduces the implementation of the operators necessary to the calculation of these fuzzy quantities. Let us recall that the purpose of this chapter is to see how taking the fuzzy quantities into account influences the implementation of these objects and the classical spatial analysis.

1.3. From the formalization of the problem to the presentation of the objects and their manipulation

Let us return to the problem thus formulated: how to estimate the quantity of product[2], in a geolocalized point X_p or a geographically limited area X_s according to its membership to one or more treatment zones of agricultural plots, knowing that there is a treatment of a certain quantity of product in ng/m^2.

First, we focus on the spatialized object: the treatment area, on which a certain amount of product has been deposited during the treatment. Several passages of treatment lead to the creation of several treated areas. In this case, it is possible to overlap treatment areas: there is then an intersection of polygons. It then respects the fact that a geolocated sector can receive several treatments as a result of overlapping during these different passages (desired or not).

As mentioned above, the difficulties of applying the treatments, particularly on the edges, mean that the geometric extension representing this area is more or less precise. We can represent by a blurred spatial object that the more we move away from the center of the treated area, the less sure it is to be part of the treated area.

The second element is that the amount of treatment used and applied is a scalar quantity that can fluctuate. It is traditionally linked to the spatialized object as a characteristic value of the area (elementary polygon) via an attribute value. Several formalisms exist to represent this error or

---

2 More simply, we will talk about the quantity of product, or more precisely the dose of active ingredient on the crop as described above in the case of agricultural plots.

misunderstanding: an interval, a confidence interval framing a value, a fuzzy number, etc. It is therefore necessary to integrate the notion of imprecision or uncertainty in this property of the object, *quantity of applied product*.

The third element focuses on the combination of these two types of fuzzy object models for the generation of new data. We speak then of merging the imprecision associated with these same geographical objects. It allows us to calculate new geographical objects or associated quantities. The operators and set operations necessary for this problem are postulated.

It is then a question of specifying for each of these elements of the selected problem: (1) its representation, by taking the notion of fuzziness into account and (2) providing the tools necessary to their handling.

1.3.1. *Materials and methods*

– A fuzzy geographic object is an extension of the definition of 1D fuzzy sets in 2D (Figure 1.2), in which a fuzzy subset A of Ω is defined by its characteristic function μ_A of Ω in $[0.1]$; $\mu_A(x)$ is the degree of membership of x to the fuzzy subset A; and x is a localized point (2D plane) of the considered geographic space. Let:

$$\{(x, \mu_A(x)), x \in A\}$$
[1.1]

– A fuzzy subset, more commonly known as a fuzzy set (equation [1.1]), can be defined by the stacking of clear sets; the α-cuts or the α-cut of a fuzzy set μ_A is the set defined by (equation [1.2]):

$$\mu_\alpha = \{x \in \Omega, \mu_A(x) \geq \alpha\}$$
[1.2]

This stacking leads to stacks of interlocking polygons of the α-cut type (Figure 1.2).

– The quantity of the treatment product is itself a fuzzy quantity represented by a fuzzy subset (Figure 1.3), which can be assimilated to a fuzzy number (Figure 1.4), a triangular fuzzy number which gives the compliance function $\mu_A(x)$ of a real quantity x to this fuzzy number A. It varies between $[0,1]$.

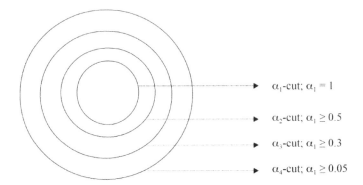

α_1-cut; $\alpha_1 = 1$

α_2-cut; $\alpha_1 \geq 0.5$

α_3-cut; $\alpha_1 \geq 0.3$

α_4-cut; $\alpha_1 \geq 0.05$

Figure 1.2. *Example of fuzzy spatial regions represented by a set of α-cuts*

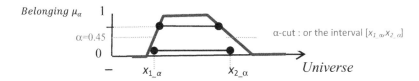

Figure 1.3. *A fuzzy subset A and its α-cuts for which $\mu_\alpha(x) \geq \alpha$. For a color version of this figure, see www.iste.co.uk/pinet/geographic2.zip*

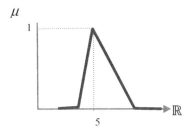

Figure 1.4. *Triangular fuzzy number. For a color version of this figure, see www.iste.co.uk/pinet/geographic2.zip*

– The quantity of product associated with a treatment area can be expressed in terms of quantity per unit area or an overall quantity. This involves (i) the calculation of the surface of the treatment area, (ii) the simultaneous occurrence of the event "the treatment took place on the plot" and the event "the quantity of product" belongs to a fuzzy interval whose compact support has only one value for a fuzzy number (Figure 1.4) and (iii) the union or the intersection between treatment areas. From the numerical representation of the vague concept associated with the fuzzy subset, the classical operations of intersection, union and complementation on these sets defines between two fuzzy subsets A and B of the same frame of reference, the membership degree of x to the intersection of A and B (Zadeh 1965). Note that the intersection becomes:

$$\mu_{A \cap B}(x) = \min\big(\mu_A(x), \mu_B(x)\big) = \mu_A(x) \wedge \mu_B(x)$$

Similarly, the union of two fuzzy numbers is defined by the maximum of the two membership functions. More generally, these two operators *min* and *max* belong, respectively, to the *t*-norms and the *t*-conorms.

Let us go back to the case of zone processing: there can either be overlapping or juxtaposition of these zones. The choice to represent each zone by a set of α-cuts enables building, for each of the sub-polygons, the degree of simultaneous membership to the plot A in blue and to the plot B n black by this ensemblistic operation. What happens at the point marked "x?", knowing that this point x? is on the two plots simultaneously? We can evaluate the value of its simultaneous membership to the two polygons, which is equal to 0.05 here (example shown in Figure 1.5).

$$\mu_{A \cap B}(x) = \min \ \mu_{A \cap B}(x?) = \ \min \ (0.3, 0.05)$$

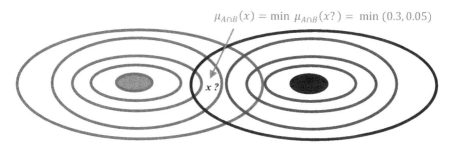

Figure 1.5. *Intersection between two fuzzy geographical areas. For a color version of this figure, see www.iste.co.uk/pinet/geographic2.zip*

$$\mu_{A \cap B}(x) = \min \Big(\mu_{\alpha_A}(x), \mu_{\alpha_B}(x)\Big) \ exemple : \ \mu_{A \cap B}(x?) = \ \min \ (0.3, 0.05)$$

– In order to integrate the notion of uncertainty to the manipulated fuzzy objects, the possibility theory models the probability of an event occurring. A measure of probability of an event A, $\Pi(A)$ is a value between 0 and 1: the maximum value 1 indicates that the event is totally possible and the value zero indicates that the event is impossible. Now the possibility of an event does not imply the impossibility of the opposite event: $\max(\Pi (A), \Pi(\bar{A})) = 1$. A totally possible event indicates that it is certain that it is possible but, unlike a probability, it does not indicate the chance that the event will occur. The notion of possibility is closely linked to fuzzy subsets, which associates the notion of imprecision and uncertainty by a possibility distribution π. When the fuzzy subset membership function is normalized, that is, $\max_{x \in X} \pi(x) = 1$, then a possibility distribution can be defined from the fuzzy set membership function; these functions not necessarily being identical. A normalized membership function has the same properties as a probability distribution. Thus, if an element has a membership degree of 0.8 to a fuzzy subset A, then the probability that v takes the value x is equal to 0.8 and its necessity is null. Thus, in the previous example if the point x? is positioned in the α-cut = 0.03 of the spatial fuzzy object processing area A: its degree of membership $\mu_A(x)$ is 0.03, and the possibility that this point x? is in A is 0.03. The necessity added to the probability provides the certainty on a fact.

– The extension principle defined by Zadeh (1965) extends the fundamental tools of classical functional relations to fuzzy quantities. Consider an application f from a universe X to another universe Y, with the fuzzy subset A defined on X. The extension principle posits that the image of f from A by $f(A)$ is a fuzzy subset of Y whose membership function is $\mu_B(y) = \sup_{x|y=f(x)} \mu_A(x)$. This principle is compatible with the use of α-cuts.

It enables us, in particular, to associate the fuzzy quantity of product used and a reliability on this fact with a treatment area. Let us take the point x? again; it belongs to the α-cut of value 0.3 (i.e. A_α) whose degree of membership is ≥ 0.3 and of equivalent probability. The quantity of product is estimated by a fuzzy number, that is, *the value of Q is around* 0.5×10^{-9} *kg/m*^{2,3} and the probability of this quantity is of maximum value, that is, 1. The principle of occurrence of these two simultaneous events A_α and Q gives that at any point x? of A_α, the product quantity is a triangular

3 The quantity Q chosen in the example is 500 ng/m². This value of 500 ng/m² is a high value in the context of the agronomy considered. A value of 200 ng/m² would be more realistic. The unit for the calculations is given in 10^{-9} kg/m².

fuzzy number around the value v whose probability is 0.3. Let us recall that the assumption is that in the α-cutting of the fuzzy spatial model of object A, the possibility is constant. In Figure 1.6, the probability of having the quantity Q at the point x? simultaneously is given by the probability $\Pi(x ?_{Ai}, Q) = 0.3$. The probability and necessity N allow us to express the certainty that the quantity is indeed between the two bounds (u^-, u^+) of the alpha cut: we are sure that the quantity Q in A_α is indeed in the interval (u^-, u^+) of the alpha cut $\alpha = 0.3$ at 70%, that is, (equal to the *min* $(1-\Pi(\notin [u^-, u^+])$; indeed, we are sure not to have a quantity less than and greater than the interval of the fuzzy number support, that is, $(a^-, a^+)_{LR}$.

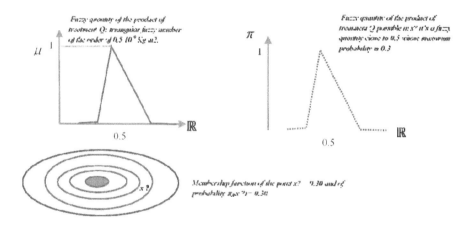

Figure 1.6. *Q possible fuzzy quantity of treatment product on an area. For a color version of this figure, see www.iste.co.uk/pinet/geographic2.zip*

The application of the extension principle to operations on fuzzy numbers such as addition, multiplication, subtraction, division is any operation * on the two fuzzy numbers, defined by:

$$\forall z \in \mathbb{R}, \mu_{A*B}(z) = \sup_{(x,y)\in\mathbb{R}^2 | x*y=z} \min[\mu_A(x), \mu_B(x)]$$

For the computations of these operators on fuzzy sets, we will adopt the parametric representation called *L-R*. Two functions of forms L (*left*) and R (*right*) defined from $\mathbb{R}^+$ in [0.1], symmetric non-decreasing on $[0; +\infty]$ with $L(0) = R(0) = 1$. A triangular or trapezoidal linear fuzzy number is then denoted by the interval list $= (a^-, a^+, \gamma^a, \beta^a)$, containing the bounds of its *support* and *core*. In terms of alpha-cutting, the arithmetic operations are obtained by arithmetic on the interval $u = (u^-, u^+)$ defined on $\mathbb{R}$ of given membership function α. For the sum and product of two fuzzy numbers in particular, we will calculate the resulting fuzzy number for the two values $\alpha = 0$ and $\alpha = 1$ associated with the bounds of the *support* (a^-, a^+) and the *core* (γ^a, β^a).

At this stage, all the methodological elements are in place to calculate both the surface of the treatment area and the quantity of treatment product used for the area. Indeed, the extension principle ensures that the surface of a treatment area will be a fuzzy number associated with the fuzzy spatial object, just as the quantity of treatment product on the whole surface will also be a fuzzy quantity.

1.3.2. Elements for the construction of manipulated fuzzy objects and their associated quantities

At this stage, we still have to consider the construction and the fuzzy representation of the three elements that are the fuzzy geographical object, that is, the treatment area; a fuzzy real quantity, that is, the quantity of product found on the area; and finally, the implementation of a spatial analysis operator (for the calculation of area and quantity/area) on fuzzy geographical objects to evaluate the total quantity of product received.

1.3.2.1. Treatment area: fuzzy geographic object A

Each treatment area A is a fuzzy spatial object composed and represented by a stack of α-cuts noted A_α: the *core* of the fuzzy spatial object corresponds to a closed polygon in which we are sure to belong to the processed area A. The possibility of being in the processed area is equal to 1. The α_i-cut is a polygon of type A_α for which the outer boundary corresponds to the value α_i of the α_i-cut, which means that any point x has the possibility of membership to $A_\alpha \geq \alpha_i$ and $\leq \alpha_{i+1}$, where α_{i+1} is the value of the α_{i+1} cut with $\alpha_{i+1} > \alpha_i$. The *t*-norm operator of *min* allows us to associate the fuzzy product quantity Q on A_α with the possibility α (see Figure 1.6).

Let us return to the stacking model of α-cuts noted A_α to represent the fuzzy spatial object A. This fuzzy representation of a spatial object is the 2D extension of a fuzzy subset, which allows us to bound its minimum and maximum degree of membership for each area, which can be simplified by associating the minimum value $\mu_{Ai}(x) = \alpha_i$ to each area, that is, a discretization of the membership function by interval. This approach is schematized in Figure 1.7. The processing area A is a fuzzy spatial object composed of a stack of α-cuts A_α: an α-cut has constant membership value α_i to A, although for any point x of this α-cut $A_{\alpha i}$ $\mu_{Ai}(x) \geq \alpha_i$. It allows for computational simplicity, although it minimizes the degree of membership and thus the possibility of membership to the area A. Its second interest is that it allows the construction of other quantities associated with the area A.

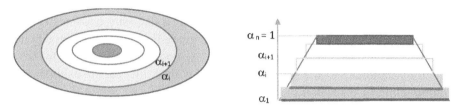

Figure 1.7. *Processing area A: the fuzzy spatial object is a stack of α-cuts A_α: an α-cut has constant membership value α_i to A, with the minimal having $\mu_{Ai}(x) \geq \alpha_i$ for the α-cut $A_{\alpha i}$. The core value $\mu_{An}(x) = 1$ is in blue and the support $\mu_{A1}(x) > 0$ but $< \mu_{Ai+1}(x)$ for i = 1..n, number of α-cuts chosen is in purple. For a color version of this figure, see www.iste.co.uk/pinet/geographic2.zip*

1.3.2.2. Calculation of the surface of the fuzzy geographic object A: the processing area

The area of the zone A is a fuzzy quantity given by a triangular fuzzy number. However, this value must be constructed from the known elements that are the different α-cuts $A_{\alpha i}$, and in particular the *core*, the α-cut with $\alpha = 0$ and the *support* α-cut with $\alpha = 1$.

Based on the *core* and the *support* of the fuzzy spatial object, a fuzzy number can be constructed. The maximum value of the *support* on $\mathbb{R}$ of this fuzzy subset is equal to the area S_sup of the contour polygon $A_{\alpha=0}$, that is, the boundary beyond which any point does not belong to the object A (polygon containing the purple area in Figure 1.7). The minimum value of the support on $\mathbb{R}$ is equal to the area S_min of the contour polygon $A_{\alpha=1}$, that is, the limit beyond which any point belongs to the object A with a confidence of 1 (blue polygon in Figure 1.7). The *core* value of the fuzzy number is a value chosen between these two bounds, which can be the average of this area or some other evaluation based on the difference between these area integrals. The total surface of A is a fuzzy quantity associated with a triangular fuzzy number (Figure 1.4), denoted as S.

1.3.2.3. *Calculation of the total amount of product possible on the treatment area, fuzzy object A, Qt*

Let Q be the quantity of product used in 10^{-9} kg/m^2, a fuzzy quantity associated here with a fuzzy triangular number. The bounds of this number are known and define the set u = (u$^-$, u$^+$), the limits of the interval on $\mathbb{R}$.

The total amount of product used on a classical (so-called *net*) geographic object bounded by the polygon of the treated area naturally becomes Q $\times$ S, where S is the area and Q is a real quantity given in 10^{-9} kg/m^2. Since Q the quantity of product is a fuzzy number, it would be necessary to have the fuzzy number S of the surface associated with A. Indeed, the extension of the principle of extension of Zadeh makes it possible to obtain the function of membership of the four arithmetic operations that are {+,-,$\times$,/}, which are necessary to the elementary calculation of the total quantity of product used in the framework of fuzzy objects. It is indeed a question of calculating a new interval $w = u \times v$, where u is the interval of the fuzzy quantity Q, v is the interval of the fuzzy quantity S and w is the interval of the total quantity Qt by using the LR model.

Let us suppose that the surface of the area A is a triangular fuzzy number with values on $\mathbb{R}$ $(1,3,3,4)_{LR}$ estimated from the two surfaces S_sup = 4 and S_min = 1 of the geometrical objects of A and Q is the quantity used, that is $(0.5,1,1,2)_{LR}$, then the Qt total quantity[4] is a fuzzy number whose value is $(0.5,3,3,8)_{LR}$ by the fuzzy multiplication as follows: $u \times v = ((uv)^-, (uv)^+)$, where the $(uv)^-$ is the minimum of the possible bounds and $(uv)^+$ is the maximum of the possible bounds of the considered α-cut. The two fuzzy numbers of respective bounds are (u^-,u^+) and (v^-,v^+), especially for the values of the *support* and the *core*. In this case, the spatial fuzzy object A is associated with fuzzy quantity Qt, which becomes an attribute of the object A in the database; Qt is not instantiated to a polygon but to the object A composed of the n α-cuts A_α. In this case, the confidence of having these values in this interval is the maximum, 100% for the treatment area A. Thus, the total quantity Qt of value = 3.0 belongs to area A, and the possibility to observe this quantity $Qt = 3.0$ is equal to 1.

---

4 Note in this example that the possible values are in 10^{-3} kg because the surface is given in km^2.

1.3.2.4. *Calculating the total amount of product possible on each α-cut $A_{\alpha i}$, the processing area A, $Qt_{\alpha i}$*

The question now is whether we can associate to an α-cut the value of the amount of product possible on its surface, that is, display how much this area could be partially processed with confidence α_i.

Similarly, the total quantity applied on each area is also associated with a triangular-type fuzzy number: to this quantity, $Qt_{\alpha i}$ is associated with the possibility α_i of having this quantity $Qt_{\alpha i}$ on $A_{\alpha i}$.

Each area is a geographical space defined by its surface with the real value: it is then difficult to consider this surface as a fuzzy quantity.

We then choose to estimate the value $Qt_{\alpha i}$ by $Qt_{\alpha i} = Q \times S_{\alpha i}$, a multiplication of a scalar – the surface $S_{\alpha i}$ and a fuzzy number Q. This arithmetic operator is defined for fuzzy numbers by the same Zadeh theorem.

The area of a concentric zone $S_{\alpha i}$ is then obtained as the difference between the area of the outer α-cut polygon $A_{\alpha i}$ with membership value α_i and the area of the α-cut polygon $A_{\alpha i+1}$ with membership value α_{i+1}. This area calculation is done by some spatial analysis and intersection operators between polygons in the vector mode.

From the area and the fuzzy quantity applied during the treatment of the plot, we obtain the total value of product possible on the α-cut. Thus, if Q the quantity used (with Q, in 10^{-9} kg/m^2) on A is defined by $(0.5; 1.1; 2)_{LR}$ and the surface is equal to 1.25 km^2, then the fuzzy multiplication by a scalar is given by: $ku = ((ku)^-, (ku)^+)$, where the $(ku)^-$ is the minimum of the possible bounds and $(ku)^+$ is the maximum of the possible bounds. Let $Qt_{\alpha i}$ be a triangular fuzzy number equal to $(0.625; 1.25; 1.25; 2.5)_{LR}$ of possibility $\Pi_{A\alpha i}(x) = \alpha_{i,}$ in this example. The possible values are in 10^{-3} kg.

Note that each quantity $Qt_{\alpha i}$ is indeed associated with an $A_{\alpha i}$. Each area is a part of the maximum extension of the fuzzy geographic object A. The union of the n areas of each zone equals the maximum possible extension of the geographic object A.

For the α-cut α_i for $i = 1$, the limit on which the value α_i is strictly different from 0 and the maximum extension is in the area A, we can calculate the estimated quantity Qt. By the properties of the fuzzy sum operator for $\alpha_{i=1}$, we find that, whatever the number n of α-cut, the support of this value is equal to the product of the area of the polygon $S_{poly_{\alpha i}=1}$, enclosing the α-cut α_i for $i = 1$ by the fuzzy value Q, that is, $(S_{\alpha i=1} + S_{\alpha i=2} + S_{\alpha i=3} \ldots S_{\alpha i=n}) \times \tilde{Q} = (S_{poly_{\alpha i}=1} \times \tilde{Q})$.

In the previous example, as the maximum surface S_sup of this polynomial is equal to 4 km^2, we obtain the number LR of the possible total quantity $(2.0; 4; 4; 8.0)_{LR}$. We cannot conclude on the possibility of observing this fuzzy quantity; we only know that it is bounded (the possibility is >0 and <1). We know that these total quantities can be at least *a little observed*, thus they are possible in the global environment of A. It then seems more interesting to determine the total quantity by alpha-cut $Qt_{\alpha i}$, fuzzy quantity whose triangular fuzzy number and probability $\Pi_{A\alpha i}(x)$ are calculable. To estimate the total quantity Qt associated with the fuzzy object A, the method to evaluate the $\otimes$ operator of two fuzzy quantities is more interesting: the most possible total processing quantity Qt is the modal value of the fuzzy number $\mu_A(x) = 1$. In the example, Qt, the total quantity on A, is a different fuzzy number $(0.5; 3; 3; 8)_{LR}$ than the one calculated by taking into account the α-cuts of the fuzzy object. The two approaches are different because they use the assumptions of constructing complementary manipulated quantities.

1.4. Implementation and storage of fuzzy objects in a relational database

In this context, we show an easily manipulated storage framework of fuzzy objects of the simple polygon without holes type. For the programmer, it is often simpler to define the fuzzy geographic object as a polygon (or ellipse) superposition without holes, and then to automatically calculate the corresponding concentric zones. Figure 1.8 can be seen as the superposition of four polygons. This geographic object could be created in the following way with PostgreSQL/PostGIS:

```
CREATE TABLE poly (tuple_id integer primary key, obj_id varchar, geom geometry,
     alpha numeric);
INSERT INTO poly VALUES (1, 'A', 'POLYGON((0 0, 100 0, 100 100, 0 100, 0 0))', 0.5);
INSERT INTO poly VALUES (2, 'A', 'POLYGON((10 10, 90 10, 90 90, 10 90, 10 10))', 0.8);
INSERT INTO poly VALUES (3, 'A', 'POLYGON((20 20, 80 20, 80 80, 20 80, 20 20))', 0.9);
INSERT INTO poly VALUES (4, 'A', 'POLYGON((45 30, 70 30, 70 70, 30 70, 45 30))', 1);
```

The object in this case is called A and is stored in the POLY table. Each tuple created in the database corresponds to a polygon without holes. Numerical "alpha" values are also indicated, which will be associated with the different concentric zones. Below, a second fuzzy object B is inserted in the table:

```
INSERT INTO poly VALUES (5, 'B', 'POLYGON((95 20, 195 20, 195 195, 95 195, 95 20))', 0.6);
INSERT INTO poly VALUES (6, 'B', 'POLYGON((105 30, 185 30, 185 185, 105 185, 105 30))', 0.7);
INSERT INTO poly VALUES (7, 'B', 'POLYGON((115 40, 175 40, 175 175, 115 175, 115 40))', 1);
```

A display can be used to automatically calculate the concentric zones of the geographic fuzzy object. It is indeed possible to order the polygons of the POLY table by fuzzy object identifier (obj_id) and by size (by area). For the polygons that have the same obj_id value, it is then sufficient to apply a spatial difference operator between the pairs of polygons that follow each other in this order. The concentric zones will then be automatically calculated. In the display below, the ord attribute corresponds to the order number calculated on the POLY table. The ST_difference function is used to calculate the spatial difference between two polygons.

```
CREATE OR REPLACE VIEW ring AS
    WITH orderedPolyByArea(ord, tuple_id, obj_id, geom, alpha) AS (
        SELECT row_number() over(), tuple_id, obj_id, geom, alpha
            FROM (SELECT tuple_id, obj_id, geom, alpha, st_area(geom) AS area
                FROM poly ORDER BY obj_id, area) AS temp)
    SELECT t1.tuple_id, t1.obj_id, t1.ord, st_difference(t1.geom, t2.geom) AS ring, t1.alpha
        FROM orderedPolyByArea t1, orderedPolyByArea t2
            WHERE t1.obj_id = t2.obj_id AND t1.ord = (t2.ord + 1);
```

Figure 1.8 shows the visualization of the areas of objects A and B, in QGIS, from the database in PostGIS. The information about a selected area appears on the right side of the figure (highlighted in red).

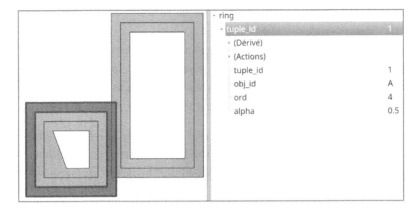

Figure 1.8. *Representation of a fuzzy geographic object. For a color version of this figure, see www.iste.co.uk/pinet/geographic2.zip*

1.5. Some examples of calculations on fuzzy objects

In this section, using some examples we show how to implement the fuzzy spatial objects presented in section 1.4. These calculations relate to the operators developed for the treatment area problem in agriculture and the quantity of product used in section 1.3.

1.5.1. *Intersection between fuzzy areas*

Two intersecting objects A and B generate intersection zones between their concentric zones. From the "alpha" values of each pair of intersecting zones, we can retrieve the minimum of these "alpha" values, as well as the geographic zone of intersection:

```
CREATE OR REPLACE VIEW ring_intersection AS
    SELECT R1.tuple_id as tuple_id_r1, R2.tuple_id as tuple_id_r2,
            LEAST(R1.alpha,R2.alpha), ST_Intersection(R1.ring,R2.ring)
    FROM ring R1, ring R2
        WHERE ST_Overlaps(R1.ring,R2.ring) and R1.tuple_id < R2.tuple_id;
```

Figure 1.9 shows a visualization of the query result (highlighted in red), superimposed on the two fuzzy objects A and B.

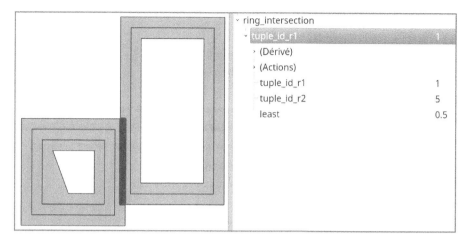

Figure 1.9. *Calculating the intersection between fuzzy areas. For a color version of this figure, see www.iste.co.uk/pinet/geographic2.zip*

1.5.2. *Amount of product associated with an α-cut of a treatment area*

If we consider that the spatial objects are agricultural plots, we can create a SPREADING table to associate a quantity of product to each concentric zone (e.g. a quantity of spread products). The quantity of products is a fuzzy number (defined by three values: vmin, vmax, vmodal). The definition of the spreading table and its values are below. The value ring_tuple_id refers to the concentric zones of the POLY table. We are only presenting here the creation of the table without the insertions of the tuples.

```
CREATE TABLE spreading (spreading_tuple_id integer primary key, ring_tuple_id integer,
        vmin numeric, vmax numeric, vmodal numeric,
        FOREIGN KEY (ring_tuple_id) REFERENCES poly(tuple_id) );
```

1.5.3. *Calculating the fuzzy surface of a fuzzy space object*

For the calculation of the fuzzy area of an object, we need to obtain the areas of its core N and its outer area E. The fuzzy area is calculated as follows: vmin = min(area of N, area of E); vmax = max(area of N, area of E); vmodal = (vmax-vmin)/2. The display below does this calculation for each object of the database.

```
CREATE OR REPLACE VIEW object_surface AS
SELECT *, (vmax-vmin)/2 as vmodal FROM (
    SELECT exte.obj_id, LEAST(exte.area, inte.area) as vmin,
            GREATEST(exte.area, inte.area) as vmax
    FROM (
            /*selection of the area of the outer zone (in the RING view) */
            SELECT obj_id, ST_AREA(ring) as area FROM ring
                WHERE ord IN (SELECT MAX(ord) FROM ring GROUP BY obj_id)) exte, (
            /*selection of the inner core area (in POLY table) */
            SELECT obj_id, ST_AREA(geom) as area FROM poly
                WHERE alpha = 1) inte
    WHERE exte.obj_id = inte.obj_id) a;
```

1.5.4. *Calculation for an α-cut of its possible product quantity using its area*

The fuzzy spread quantities are stored in the SPREADING table. For each zone, we can calculate the fuzzy quantity of spread product, which is a fuzzy number composed of three values calculated as follows:

– vmin = area of the zone * minimum value of the quantities;

– vmax = area of the zone * maximum value of the quantities;

– vmodal = area of the zone * modal value of the quantities.

The query below shows how to apply this calculation on the fields of the RING display:

```
SELECT tuple_id, ST_AREA(ring)*vmin as vmin_q, ST_AREA(ring)*vmax as vmax_q,
        ST_AREA(ring)*vmodal as vmodal_q
    FROM spreading, ring
        WHERE ring_tuple_id=tuple_id;
```

The calculation of the total quantity of product is applied considering that this quantity is a fuzzy quantity of a fuzzy spatial object P.

It is possible to have a table storing a fuzzy quantity of products for each object:

```
CREATE TABLE object_qtit (obj_id varchar primary key, vmin numeric, vmax numeric,
    vmodal numeric);
```

From the data in the OBJECT_QTIT and OBJECT_SURFACE tables, we can then calculate the three values that make up the total quantity of products of the entire space object:

- object_qtit_tot.vmin =

  Min(object_qtit.vmin * object_surface.vmin ,

  object_qtit.vmin * object_surface.vmax,

  object_qtit.vmax * object_surface.vmin,

  object_qtit.vmax * object_surface.vmax)

- object_qtit_tot.vmax =

  Max(object_qtit.vmin * object_surface.vmin ,

  object_qtit.vmin * object_surface.vmax,

  object_qtit.vmax * object_surface.vmin,

  object_qtit.vmax * object_surface.vmax)

- object_qtit_tot.vmodal = object_qtit.vmodal * object_surface.vmodal

This calculation can be done with the following OBJECT_QTIT_TOT display:

```
CREATE VIEW object_qtit_tot AS
    SELECT object_qtit.obj_id,
        LEAST(object_qtit.vmin * object_surface.vmin,
            object_qtit.vmin * object_surface.vmax,
            object_qtit.vmax * object_surface.vmin,
            object_qtit.vmax * object_surface.vmax) as vmin,
```

```
GREATEST(object_qtit.vmin * object_surface.vmin,

          object_qtit.vmin * object_surface.vmax,

          object_qtit.vmax * object_surface.vmin,

          object_qtit.vmax * object_surface.vmax) as vmax,

     object_qtit.vmodal * object_surface.vmodal as vmodal

FROM object_qtit, object_surface WHERE object_qtit.obj_id=object_surface.obj_id;
```

Figure 1.10 shows an example of visualization of the calculated data in QGIS. The visualization is produced by joining the POLY table and the OBJECT_QTIT_TOT data.

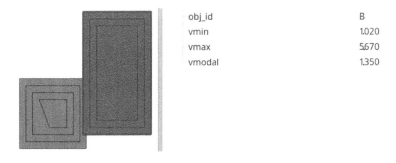

obj_id	B
vmin	1.020
vmax	5.670
vmodal	1.350

Figure 1.10. *Visualization of the total quantity of an object. For a color version of this figure, see www.iste.co.uk/pinet/geographic2.zip*

1.5.5. *Going further*

– These few elements make it possible to consider the qualification of a quantity of treatment product on a treatment area, which is imprecise without integrating the dimension of vague objects in this case.

– They answer the question as to how elementary surface calculation functions in particular can be considered for fuzzy spatial objects (Stefanini et al. 2016). Although this question is very elementary in the case of classical spatial analysis, a systematic formula for fuzzy spatial objects is not available.

– The question of length on a linear spatial object must be integrated if we try to take the path taken by the tractor into account. It requires us to consider the estimation of a fuzzy length knowing that the polyline of the path object is deterministic in a spatial database (Dilo 2006).

– These elements take into account the calculation of the exposure of a geographical area partially covered by two successive treatment zones, partial membership to zone A1 and partial membership to zone A2, and applying a quantity Q1 and a quantity Q2 estimated in an imprecise way (Zayrit 2015). This involves combining the steps of (i) calculating for an α-cut its possible product quantity using its area and (ii) the intersection between two fuzzy areas. It can be generalized to the intersection of order greater than 2.

– The integration of both fuzzy boundaries and uncertainty, as in the consideration of the path of the treatment vehicle on the plot, opens up the perspective of considering the so-called vague spatial objects.

1.6. Conclusion

This chapter aimed to illustrate the implementation and manipulation of the concepts of imprecision and uncertainty within the framework of fuzzy spatial objects (poorly known limits) with an illustrative case of application in agronomy. The problem of assigning a total quantity to a polygonal surface object, although elementary, requires a reformulation of the problem and reasoning to propagate some classical arithmetic operators. It shows how the principle of Zadeh (1965) can be generalized even if there is no analytical formulation of this theorem. This theorem allows us to consider the fusion of several types of imprecision and uncertainty, especially in the second problem where we have to integrate the path of the vehicle, which becomes a fuzzy linear spatial object or a probability of passage or not. Finally, the chapter proposes an implementation of this type of approach in a classical database and query system. The given examples allow us to see in practice how it is possible to implement the presented approach concretely, with freely available tools (PostgreSQL and QGIS). The described experimentation shows that it is possible to implement the approach quite directly and easily. Nevertheless, we did not evaluate the performance of the queries and the proposed structures in the case of large volumes of spatial data. Note that the use of materialized views can be used for performance reasons.

We have illustrated our modeling and calculations on a case in agriculture. We took the example of the treatment of an agricultural plot represented by a fuzzy spatial object composed of a central part where the applied dose corresponds to the recommendations of use. A peripheral uncertain spatial extension receives a lower dose. The dose received by the crop can also be represented by a fuzzy number. In this example, the complete modeling implies looking at the n treatments done during the year. During the season, the crop evolves from the seedling stage to the "adult" plant stage with, for some crops (e.g. maize), a consequent increase in the leaf mass. Correlatively, the dose of active ingredient on the plant increases with the growth of the crop and therefore with time. The underlying modeling question is: How do we represent this temporal evolution? This type of modeling becomes even more complex in the context of agri-environmental monitoring of farms because the crop plots can be subdivided, grouped, etc., according to the rotations, but also in order to put in crops with higher added value or better respond to market needs.

1.7. References

Batton-Hubert, M., Desjardin, E., Pinet. F. (2019). *Geographic Data Imperfection 1: From Theory to Applications*. ISTE Ltd, London, and John Wiley & Sons, New York.

Dilo, A. (2006). Representation of and reasoning with vagueness in spatial information. A system for handling vague objects. Thesis, International Institute for Geo-information Science & Earth Observation (ITC), Enschede, The Netherlands.

Stefanini, L., Sorini, M., Letizia Guerra, M. (2016). *Fuzzy Numbers and Fuzzy Arithmetic in Handbook of Granular Computing*. John Wiley & Sons, Hoboken.

Zadeh., L.A. (1965). Fuzzy sets. *Information and Control*, 8, 338–353.

Zadeh, L.A. (1978). Fuzzy sets as a basis for a theory of possibility. *Fuzzy Sets and Systems*, 1, 3–28.

Zayrit, K. (2015). Fusion des données imparfaites multi-sources : application à la spatialisation qualifiée des pratiques agricoles. PhD Thesis, Université de Reims Champagne-Ardennes, Reims.

Zayrit, K., Desjardin, E., de Runz, C., Akdag, H. (2011). Propagation of spatial imprecision in imprecise quantitative data in agronomy. *International Symposium on Spatial Data Quality (ISSDQ)*, Coimbra.

Representation and Analysis of the Evolution of Agricultural Territories by a Spatio-temporal Graph

The evolution of land use in agricultural areas is closely linked to environmental problems such as the pollution of water resources or soil erosion involving muddy water flows. It is therefore important to monitor and anticipate these developments on a regional scale. The Land Parcel Identification System (LPIS) is a source of information, which has recently been made available to the public, that allows such monitoring, provided that adequate analysis tools are available and adapted to the characteristics of these data, particularly their spatiotemporal characteristics. It is the development of such tools that we have undertaken, by coupling a representation of the data by a fuzzy spatiotemporal graph and a method for mining frequent sub-graphs, bringing to light the main spatiotemporal characteristics of the crops in a selected region.

2.1. The data: the land parcel identification system

The LPIS is a geographic database which was set up by France to meet the European Union's requirement for all of its Member States to locate and identify farm fields in return for aid paid under the Common Agricultural

Chapter written by Aurélie LEBORGNE, Ezriel STEINBERG, Florence LE BER and Stella MARC-ZWECKER.

Policy. The LPIS covers all French departments (except Mayotte) as well as the overseas collectivities of Saint-Barthélemy and Saint-Martin. An excerpt from the LPIS for the Department of Somme is shown in Figure 2.1.

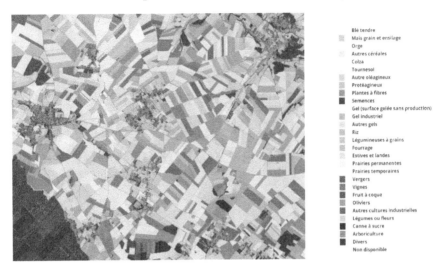

Blé tendre
Maïs grain et ensilage
Orge
Autres céréales
Colza
Tournesol
Autre oléagineux
Protéagineux
Plantes à fibres
Semences
Gel (surface gelée sans production)
Gel industriel
Autres gels
Riz
Légumineuses à grains
Fourrage
Estives et landes
Prairies permanentes
Prairies temporaires
Vergers
Vignes
Fruit à coque
Oliviers
Autres cultures industrielles
Légumes ou fleurs
Canne à sucre
Arboriculture
Divers
Non disponible

Figure 2.1. *Extract from the 2019 edition of the LPIS for the Somme (Crécy-en-Ponthieu and its surroundings) © IGN 2021. For a color version of this figure, see www.iste.co.uk/pinet/geographic2.zip*

The LPIS was set up in 2002 and compiles data from the agricultural area declarations made each year by the farmers themselves. Thus, every year, each farmer must draw and update the crop blocks (up to 2014), then the crop fields (since 2015, version 2.0) that they farm and declare the crops grown there and their surfaces.

The version released as part of the public reference data service is anonymized. The attributes contained in version 2.0 of the LPIS and associated with each field are as follows:

– a unique identifier for the field (ID_PARCEL);

– a code to identify the main crop on the field (CODE_CULTU);

– a code to identify which crop group the field is associated with (CODE_GROUP);

– two codes to identify catch crops, that is, crops intercropped between two main crops (CULTURE_D1 and CULTURE_D2). This information is not used in the following.

Although the LPIS is a valuable source of information on the status and evolution of land use and field pattern, it must be used with caution because this information is subject to uncertainty for several reasons: absence of certain agricultural surfaces (surfaces for which there is no aid), variability from one year to the next (changes in aid, surfaces not declared for a reason related to a given farm's activity), modifications made by the farmer even though there is no change on the ground, etc. In addition, the data from the LPIS are subject to the inaccuracies that characterize geographic databases. In particular, polygons that represent the same field on two different dates may be slightly off.

LPIS data have been used for various studies in the agronomic field, in particular, the LPIS Explorer tool has been developed specifically to facilitate analysis [LEV 16].

2.2. The model: a fuzzy spatiotemporal graph

2.2.1. *Graph structure*

In this work, we rely on the spatiotemporal graph model proposed by [DEL 10], a model that allows us to represent the spatial and temporal evolutions of spatial entities. A spatiotemporal graph is a multigraph, defined as the union of three oriented subgraphs:

1) The graph of spatial relations characterizes spatially the interactions between entities at a given time. It is composed of nodes and arcs in green (EC labels), as shown in Figure 2.2.

2) The spatiotemporal relations graph exploits the same relations as the spatial relations graph, but considers entities at different times. It is composed of nodes and arcs in red (labels TPP, TPPi), as shown in Figure 2.2.

3) The graph of the relations of filiation, defined on the concept of identity, makes it possible to characterize the transmission of the identity through time. It is composed of nodes and arcs in blue (labels δ, γ), as shown in Figure 2.2.

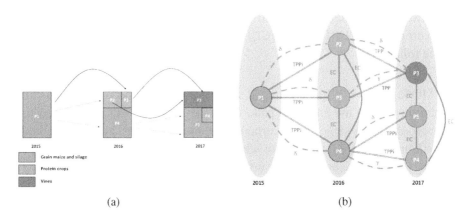

(a)   (b)

Figure 2.2. *(a) Example of the evolution of an agricultural territory between 2015 and 2017: (b) spatiotemporal graph modeling (a) spatial and spatiotemporal arcs labeled by the relations of the RCC8 theory, filiation arcs by specific labels. For a color version of this figure, see www.iste.co.uk/pinet/geographic2.zip*

2.2.2. *Spatial relationships*

In the following, we will consider that each spatial entity A (parcel) is composed of an interior A^o, a boundary δA and an exterior A^e. The eight basic relations of the RCC8 theory [RAN 92] describe in an exhaustive and disjointed way (only one relation is checked) the relative position of two such entities. This theory is based on the notion of connection, where two entities are connected if they share at least one point. These relationships are computed on the geographic data as the combination of the results of the intersections of the interiors, exteriors and boundaries of the involved features [EGE 92]. Two regions A and B are disconnected (DC relation) if the intersection of their borders, as well as their interiors, is empty (but the exterior of A contains the interior of B and vice versa). They are connected externally (they are in contact, relation EC) if the intersection of their borders is non-empty, while the intersection of their interiors is empty. They partially overlap (relation PO) if neither the intersection of the borders nor the intersection of the interiors is empty, as well as the intersection of the exterior of each region with the interior of the other (see Figure 2.3).

Note that the DC relationship is implicitly represented in the graph by the absence of an arc. To enrich the model, and to take into account the particularities of the LPIS data (plots do not always touch each other, they are separated by paths, roads or hedges), we added proximity relations, which are based on the definition of a distance between two entities, measured as the minimum of the Euclidean distances $d(x, y)$ between all of the points x and y of the two entity boundaries.

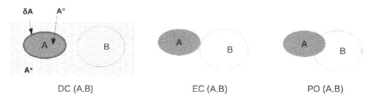

DC (A,B)   EC (A,B)   PO (A,B)

Figure 2.3. *The DC, EC and PO relations between two regions A and B*

DEFINITION 2.1.– Let A and B be two parcels, the distance between A and B is defined by $d(A, B) = min_{x \in \delta A, y \in \delta B} \, d(x, y)$

On this basis, we distinguish two types of proximity relationships, an absolute proximity and a proximity relative to the size of the plots [LEB 19b]. The absolute proximity relationship links two parcels within a distance b of each other (separated by a ditch, or a road for example). In our study, $b = 2$ m. Plots A and B are *absolutely close* $(p_a(A, B))$ if and only if:

$$0 < d(A, B) \leq b \qquad\qquad [2.1]$$

The relative proximity relationship makes it possible to connect one field to another if their distance respects a threshold proportional to the area of the second. Formally, the field A is *relatively close* to B, $(p_r(A, B))$ if and only if:

$$0 < d(A, B) \leq \frac{\sqrt{R_B}}{N} \qquad\qquad [2.2]$$

where R_B is the area of plot B and N is a given number. Note that this relationship is not symmetrical. In our experiments, we used two values of N (10 and 15), allowing us to define two relative proximities. For $N = 10$, for example, if B is a 4 acre parcel, then parcels located within 20 m of B will be considered as close.

Calculating these three proximity relations, in addition to the EC and PO relations, allows us to consider different situations and to better account for the notion of proximity.

2.2.3. *Spatiotemporal relationships*

Concerning the spatiotemporal relations, and to take into account the uncertainties specific to the data, we use the fuzzy variant of the RCC8 relations introduced by [CLE 97], where the entities are endowed with a thick border, noted ΔA. Each relation is then presented in different configurations, as shown in Figure 2.5 for the relation EC (see [LEB 19a]).

Concretely, the original borders of the plots are thickened on both sides of a fixed ϵ value (see Figure 2.4), which enables the use of the fuzzy relations model for plots at two successive dates.

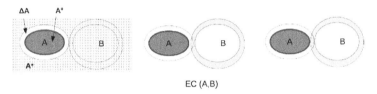

EC (A,B)

Figure 2.4. *The different configurations of the EC relationship for regions with thick borders*

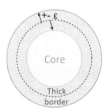

Figure 2.5. *Thickening of the boundary of a parcel on both sides of the original boundary. For a color version of this figure, see www.iste.co.uk/pinet/geographic2.zip*

2.2.4. *Relationships of filiation*

Two types of relationships of filiation[1] are discerned, consistent with the model described by [DEL 10]:

---

1 The identity of a parcel is described in the LPIS, and is maintained from one edition of the LPIS to the next (for post-2015 editions), when the geometry of the parcel is not changed.

– The continuation: two parcels A and B are in a continuation relation if A and B have the same identity, that is, they are the same entity but at different times. An entity can have at most one continuation relation (see the γ in Figure 2.2).

– The derivation: two parcels A and B are in a derivation relationship if B derives from A and potentially from other entities. Some of the information contained by A is present in B (see the δ relations in Figure 2.2).

Note that for pattern mining, these relationships will not be used because, in the context of the LPIS data, they cover most of the information carried by spatiotemporal relationships.

2.3. The method: searching for frequent patterns

2.3.1. *Overview*

Frequent pattern mining is a field of research that has developed since the 1990s [AGR 94]. It consists of searching for recurrences in a set of data, tables, texts, time series or graphs. The number of repetitions of a pattern, or in other words, the number of objects that bear this pattern, is called support. A pattern is said to be frequent if its support is greater than a given threshold. In the context of graphs, a frequent pattern is a subgraph, which is therefore identical to several other subgraphs (same number of nodes, connected by the same arcs, the graphs are said to be isomorphic (see Figure 2.6)) within a general graph.

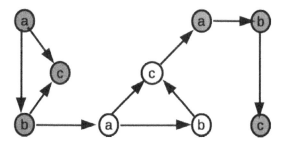

Figure 2.6. *Three subgraphs (blue, yellow, red) in a graph G: the blue and yellow subgraphs are isomorphic. For a color version of this figure, see www.iste.co.uk/pinet/geographic2.zip*

Formally, we note $G = (V, E)$ a simple graph, with V the set of vertices (nodes) and $E \subseteq V \times V$ the set of arcs (or edges in the case of an undirected graph). A subgraph of G, $G' = (V', E')$ is such that $V' \subset V$ and $E' = V' \times V' \cap E$. Two graphs $G_1 = (V_1, E_1)$, $G_2 = (V_2, E_2)$ are isomorphic if there exists a bijection f of V_1 to V_2, such that a pair of vertices (u, v) of G_1 is an arc of G_1 if and only if the pair $(f(u), f(v))$ is an arc of G_2.

2.3.2. *Methods for subgraph mining*

There are different methods for finding frequent subgraphs in a given graph: the approach proposed by [INO 00] is based on the Apriori algorithm, developed for the search of simple patterns [AGR 94]. Other approaches have been proposed, for example, by [KUR 01] and [YAN 02], but only one to our knowledge allows us to mine the subgraphs of a multigraph such as the spatiotemporal graph. It is thus the algorithm MuGRaM [ING 18] that we have used, after having adapted it to oriented labeled multigraphs. The adapted algorithm, LD-MuGRaM, supports both arc and node labels. The principle of this algorithm is briefly described below. For more information, see [LEB 22].

The general operation is based on the monotonicity property of frequency, that is, the subgraphs of a frequent subgraph are also frequent, while the subgraphs containing a non-frequent subgraph are non-frequent. This builds the subgraphs by assembling small frequent subgraphs until obtaining a non-frequent subgraph where the process stops. The algorithm therefore starts by searching for two-node subgraphs, by enumerating the arcs, and retains those that are repeated beyond a given threshold support α. These subgraphs are assembled to create larger subgraphs. At each step, the frequency of the current subgraph is evaluated by searching for subgraphs that are isomorphic to it, whose total number must be greater than the threshold α.

2.4. Characterizing agricultural regions by spatial-temporal patterns

We tested our approach on four datasets from different regions of France (Figure 2.7). For each region, we extracted a graph of about 10,000 nodes covering 5 years (from 2015 to 2019), or about 2,000 nodes per temporality. In this experiment, the relationships were generalized and simplified to one spatial type (neighbor) and one spatiotemporal type (equality: EQ). In fact, only the plots that are stable in time (no merging or splitting) are linked.

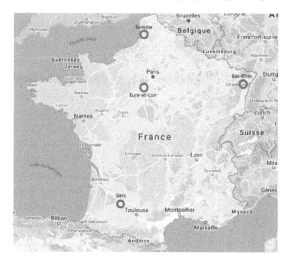

Figure 2.7. *Location of the studied areas (Google Maps background©). For a color version of this figure, see www.iste.co.uk/pinet/geographic2.zip*

Table 2.1 shows the characteristics of the graphs in number of nodes and arcs, as well as the main crops present (above 6%) in the node labels. These percentages represent the land uses in number of plots and not in area. Each dataset is named by the corresponding department.

Table 2.1 calls for the following remarks:

– The number of leading crops in each region varies: the dataset extracted from Bas–Rhin contains mainly monocultures, the dataset extracted from Gers has two main crops involved in the same rotation [JOU 11, XIA 14], the dataset extracted from Somme has grasslands and the dataset extracted from Eure-et-Loir is the most diversified.

– The number of spatial relations is stable, relative to the number of nodes, which is related to the fact that the number of neighboring parcels is constrained by their shapes, which are generally regular.

– The number of spatiotemporal relationships is highly variable (compared to the expected average of 8,000), particularly low for the Gers and

Eure-et-Loir data: this is undoubtedly due to field rearrangements and the specifications of the LPIS data collection.

Department	Number of nodes	Number of spatial arcs	Number of time arcs	Majority crops (% nodes)
Gers	10.743	83.317	2.018	Soft winter wheat 15.2% Fallow land for 6 years 14.8% Sunflowers 14.1% Buffer strip 7.5%
Bas-Rhin	9.810	82.541	6.922	Wine grape vine 57.3% Maize silage 23.6% Soft winter wheat 7.3%
Eure-et-Loir	10.866	89.246	3.601	Soft winter wheat 21.4% Winter rapeseed 10.4% Hard winter wheat 8.9% Fallow land for 6 years 6.9% Temp. not exploited area 6.7% Spring barley 6.6% Corn 6.2%
Somme	12.196	87.659	6.353	Soft winter wheat 24.4% Permanent pasture 19.7% Maize silage 9.8% Temp. not exploited area 7.0% Non-fodder beet 6.9%

Table 2.1. *Characteristics of graphs for each region studied*

Finally, the different characteristics of the data sets will lead to different computation times when searching for patterns.

The method we use allows the extraction of any pattern, whether temporal, spatial or spatiotemporal. As we are mainly interested in the latter, which are not the most frequent, we force their extraction by eliminating patterns that do not have both spatial (neighbor) and spatiotemporal (EQ) relations. In the following, however, we also present patterns without spatial relations.

2.4.1. *Data from Gers*

For the Gers graph (10,743 nodes), a threshold support of 40 was used. Two examples of frequent patterns are shown in Figure 2.8. Each pattern consists of a set of four nodes on two temporalities, which appear, at least, 40 times in the graph. These two patterns highlight the successions soft winter wheat-soft winter wheat (Figure 2.8(a)) and soft winter wheat-sunflower (Figure 2.8(b)) and their co-location: two neighboring wheat plots continue to be planted with wheat the following year, or are planted with sunflowers. These two configurations are part of a crop rotation involving wheat and sunflowers that is very present in the southwest, alongside corn monocultures.

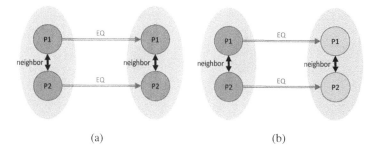

(a)   (b)

Figure 2.8. *Examples of frequent patterns found for the Gers: in blue, soft winter wheat, in yellow/orange, sunflower. For a color version of this figure, see www.iste.co.uk/pinet/geographic2.zip*

2.4.2. *Data from Bas-Rhin*

Concerning the graph (9,810 nodes) from the Bas-Rhin data, we notice in Table 2.1 that the nodes representing wine grape plots are in the majority (57.3%): the chosen zone, straddling the Vosges foothills and the Alsace plain, also includes corn plots (23.6% of the nodes), but they are much larger and therefore less numerous than the vineyard plots for an equivalent overall surface. Moreover, these two crops are monocultures, which generates very little spatial and temporal variability.

Because of these particularities, the computation time of the patterns – which can be large when the support decreases – is important, which led us to choose a very high threshold support[2] of 4,000. With this threshold support, we find the pattern presented in Figure 2.9, which characterizes the Piedmont area where the neighboring plots keep the same vine crop for several years.

---

2 Note that the sub-graphs counted for a pattern can overlap.

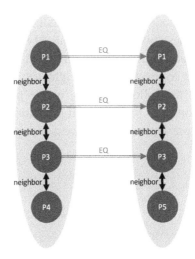

Figure 2.9. *Example of a pattern found for the Bas-Rhin: in purple, vines for wine grapes. For a color version of this figure, see www.iste.co.uk/pinet/geographic2.zip*

2.4.3. *Data from Eure-et-Loir*

For the data concerning the Eure-et-Loir (graph of 10,866 nodes), we were able to use a threshold support of 40 because the crops are quite varied: soft winter wheat is in the majority (21.4%), followed by rapeseed (10.4%) and hard winter wheat (8.9%); fallow land, uncultivated areas and other crops also appear (see Table 2.1). Figure 2.10 shows some examples of the patterns obtained for these majority crops. The pattern in Figure 2.10(a) is representative of the crop rotations involving rapeseed and soft winter wheat, which are typical of this region. The patterns of Figures 2.10(b), 2.10(c) and 2.10(d) highlight the long fallows and temporarily uncultivated areas of this cash crop territory.

2.4.4. *Data from the Somme*

The graph contains 12,196 nodes. The main crops are soft winter wheat (24.4%), then silage maize (9.8%) and sugar beet (6.9%). Permanent grasslands are very present (19.7%). Temporarily unexploited surfaces are also present. In the search for patterns, the nodes labeled "grassland", which generate long temporal patterns, were eliminated. The patterns obtained with a threshold support of 40, examples of which are shown in Figure 2.11, therefore contain only crops or unharvested areas.

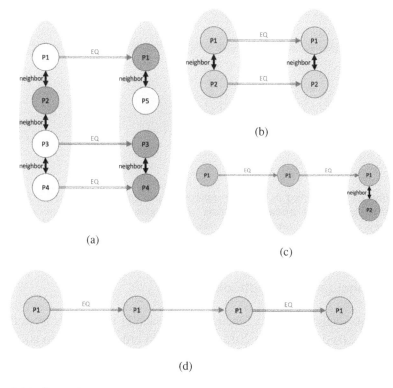

Figure 2.10. *Examples of frequent patterns found for the Eure-et-Loir: in blue, soft winter wheat; in yellow, rapeseed; in light green, fallow land of 6 years or more; in gray, temporarily unused areas. For a color version of this figure, see www.iste.co.uk/pinet/geographic2.zip*

These patterns reflect wheat-based crop rotations: here wheat-maize (patterns in Figures 2.11(a) and 2.11(d)) and wheat-beet (patterns in Figures 2.11(b) and 2.11(c)), characteristic of the cultivated plateaus of northern France [XIA 14]. As for the Eure-et-Loir data, we observe areas that have not been farmed for several years, in the vicinity of wheat-based rotations (pattern in Figure 2.11(e)).

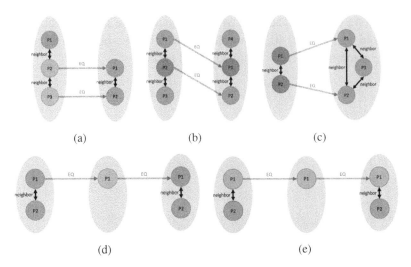

Figure 2.11. *Examples of frequent patterns found for the Somme (Ponthieu region): in blue, soft winter wheat; in fuchsia, non-fodder beet; in mauve, silage maize; in gray, temporarily uncultivated areas. For a color version of this figure, see www.iste.co.uk/pinet/geographic2.zip*

2.5. Conclusion and outlook

In this chapter, we have focused on modeling farm fields from the LPIS (version 2.0) data between 2015 and 2019. In order to take into account both the spatial and temporal aspects, we have used a spatiotemporal graph model [DEL 10]. We then sought to extract relevant information from these data. To do so, we adapted a multigraph frequent pattern mining algorithm [ING 18] to the characteristics of spatiotemporal graphs.

Although this algorithm has an exponential complexity, we were able to extract frequent patterns on areas of interest of about 2,000 agricultural plots evolving over 5 years. In order to limit the complexity of the graphs, we only considered a spatial relationship of proximity and a spatial-temporal relationship of equality. Despite this, and depending on the characteristics of the datasets, the search for patterns can be very costly.

On the four processed datasets, we were able to extract frequent patterns that take into account both the spatial and temporal component. It would obviously be possible to treat the spatial and temporal aspects separately with the same algorithm, but there are other more efficient tools, especially for the study of temporal sequences, such as Markov models [MAR 11].

As this work is a first approach to mining frequent patterns in a spatiotemporal graph modeling agricultural plots, we consider several perspectives. Firstly, it would be interesting to use more distant spatial relations to find patterns at a slightly larger scale (involving plots one plot away). In this case, each node will have more relations, the graph will be denser, which will increase the computation time. Another perspective could be to group some of the crops together to obtain more general patterns, such as patterns involving wheat and another crop (beet, peas, etc.). More broadly, it will be interesting to introduce in the algorithm an option to group similar patterns, in order to extract more patterns, but which would be, to some extent, approximate.

2.6. References

[AGR 94] AGRAWAL R., SRIKANT R., "Fast algorithms for mining association rules", *Proceedings of the 20th VLDB Conference*, pp. 487–499, 1994.

[CLE 97] CLEMENTINI E., DI FELICE P., "Approximate topological relations", *International Journal of Approximate Reasoning*, vol. 16, no. 2, pp. 173–204, 1997.

[DEL 10] DEL MONDO G., STELL J.G., CLARAMUNT C., et al., "A graph model for spatio-temporal evolution", *Journal of Universal Computer Science*, vol. 16, pp. 1452–1477, 2010.

[EGE 92] EGENHOFER M.J., AL-TAHA K.K., "Reasoning about gradual changes of topological relationships", in FRANK A.U., CAMPARI I., FORMENTINI U. (eds), *Theories and Methods of Spatio-temporal Reasoning in Geographic Space*, Springer, Berlin, Heidelberg, 1992.

[ING 18] INGALALLI V., IENCO D., PONCELET P., "Mining frequent subgraphs in multigraphs", *Information Sciences*, vol. 04, pp. 451–452, 2018.

[INO 00] INOKUCHI A., WASHIO T., MOTODA H., "An apriori-based algorithm for mining frequent substructures from graph data", *PKDD 2000, Principles of Data Mining and Knowledge Discovery*, pp. 13–23, 2000.

[JOU 11] JOUY L., WISSOCQ A., "Observatoire des pratiques, 34 types de successions culturales en France", *Perspectives agricoles*, vol. 379, pp. 44–46, 2011.

[KUR 01] KURAMOCHI M., KARYPIS G., "Frequent subgraph discovery", *Proceedings of IEEE International Conference on Data Mining*, pp. 313–320, 2001.

[LEB 19a] LE BER F., "Algebraic reasoning for uncertain data", in BATTON-HUBERT M., DESJARDIN E., PINET F. (eds), *Geographic Data Imperfection 1: From Theory to Applications*, ISTE Ltd, London, and John Wiley & Sons, New York, 2019.

[LEB 19b] LEBORGNE A., MEYER A., GIRAUD H., et al., "Un graphe spatio-temporel pour modéliser l'évolution de parcelles agricoles", *Conférence SAGEO*, Clermont-Ferrand, 2019.

[LEB 22] LEBORGNE A., STEINBERG E., LAFONTAINE L., et al., "Recherche de motifs fréquents dans un multi-graphe étiqueté orienté", *Soumis à la Conférence EGC*, 2022.

[LEV 16] LEVAVASSEUR F., MARTIN P., BOUTY C., et al., "RPG explorer: A new tool to ease the analysis of agricultural landscape dynamics with the Land Parcel Identification System", *Computers and Electronics in Agriculture*, vol. 127, pp. 541–552, 2016.

[MAR 11] MARI J.-F., LE BER F., LAZRAK E.-G., et al., "Using Markov models to mine temporal and spatial data", in FUNATSU K., HASEGAWA K. (eds), *New Fundamental Technologies in Data Mining*, Intech, London, 2011.

[RAN 92] RANDELL D.A., CUI Z., COHN A.G., "A spatial logic based on regions and connection", *Proceedings of the 3rd International Conference on Knowledge Representation and Reasoning*, Morgan Kaufmann Publishers, San Mateo, 1992.

[XIA 14] XIAO Y., MIGNOLET C., MARI J.-F., et al., "Modeling the spatial distribution of crop sequences at a large regional scale using land-cover survey data: A case from France", *Computers and Electronics in Agriculture*, vol. 102, pp. 51–63, 2014.

[YAN 02] YAN X., HAN J., "gSpan: graph-based substructure pattern mining", *Proceedings of the IEEE International Conference on Data Mining*, pp. 721–724, 2002.

3

Agricultural Areas in the Face of Public Environmental Policies: Spatiotemporal Analyses Using Sensitive Data

The analysis of the effects of public environmental policies (PEPs) on agricultural areas at the fine scale of the plot or farm involves so-called "sensitive" data. The objective of the FARMaine (*Foncier, Aménagement et Régulations dans le bassin de la Maine* or Land tenure and regulation in the Maine River Basin) project was to analyze these effects but also to disseminate the results through a tool called FarmSIG (Follin et al. 2021). Thus, the question arises of the means that can be mobilized to disseminate results from sensitive data while respecting the confidentiality of the information. The approach we present here consists of voluntarily introducing a degree of uncertainty into the information before it can be published.

For this purpose, we propose two approaches: the first one, based on spatial aggregation by gridding, makes the location of farms uncertain, and the second one, based on thematic aggregation by classification, makes the characterization of agricultural plots uncertain.

After presenting the FARMaine project and our questions, we will present a brief inventory of existing methods for the deliberate introduction of imperfections into data from the semantic point of view, on the one hand, and from the spatial point of view, on the other hand. We will then present the data on which we have relied and show which concern both agricultural

Chapter written by Jean-Michel FOLLIN, Nathalie THOMMERET and Marie FOURNIER.

activity and land, before detailing the treatments that we have applied to them at the farm level (calculation of indicators of spatial structure and intensity of agro-environmental measures, then gridding) and at the plot level (classification of land changes in order to define a typology).

3.1. Project context and issues

The issue of monitoring agricultural territories where PEPs are implemented, in particular the consequences of these policies on the functioning of farms and the management of agricultural land, is of primary importance for the public actors in charge.

The FARMaine project, conducted within the framework of the national PSDR4 program (*Pour et Sur le Développement Régional* or For and about regional development) and adapted to the scale of the Grand Ouest region, has set itself the objective of shedding light on the modalities of implementation of the PEPs in the valley bottom areas of the Maine River Basin (Fournier 2016). More specifically, we attempt to provide answers to the following questions: Are there changes in the agricultural and land profile of the areas studied? Can we establish a link between spatial structures of the farms and the presence of PEPs?

To do this, various treatments (cross-referencing, statistical analysis) were conducted on spatial data covering different dates (between 2009 and 2018), themes (land, agricultural, regulatory) and scales (farms and agricultural plots). Four study territories were selected to conduct our studies, allowing us to cover a diversity of situations in terms of environmental issues, the presence of PEPs and agricultural systems observed. These are the Basses-Vallées Angevines (BVA), the Alpes Mancelles, the Vallée du Loir and the Oudon watershed (Figure 3.1).

A web-GIS, named FarmSIG, has been developed to gather and disseminate the data and analyses produced in the framework of the FARMaine project. It aims to provide a synthetic cartographic vision of the valley bottom areas studied and keys to understanding their characteristics and their evolution in relation to the PEPs. FarmSIG is intended for various user profiles (farmers, agents of Chambers of Agriculture, researchers in agronomy, planning and geography).

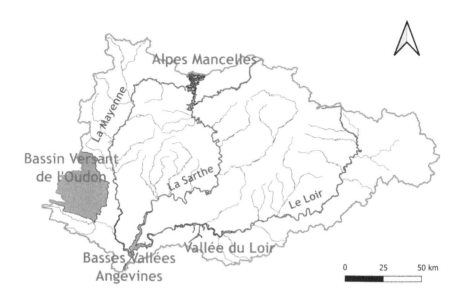

Figure 3.1. *The four study areas of the FARMaine project in the Maine River Basin. For a color version of this figure, see www.iste.co.uk/pinet/geographic2.zip*

The mapped results were voluntarily degraded because they are calculated from data that are protected, as we will see in section 3.3: the Land Parcel Identification System (LPIS) level 2, the Agro-environmental and Climate Measures (AECM) and the Land files. The voluntary degradation of data before disseminating them corresponds to so-called controlled uncertainty (Follin et al. 2019) carried out here with the objective of respecting privacy and business secrecy.

This controlled uncertainty makes it possible to prevent the reconstruction of farms by identifying the plots belonging to the same owner and the precise location of elements (farms on which AECMs are applied and land characteristics of the plots). It is therefore comparable to a form of anonymization.

Indeed, anonymization is described, according to ISO 29100, as "the process by which personally identifiable information (PII) is irreversibly altered in such a way that the subject of the PII can no longer be identified directly or indirectly, either by the controller of the PII alone or in collaboration with any other party".

The basic question that drives the work of FarmSIG is therefore the following: How to report on trends or trajectories of the evolution of farms and plots in relation to PEPs without revealing PII?

3.2. What are the methods for anonymization?

The anonymization of geographic information can affect either its attribute component or its spatial component.

3.2.1. *For the attributes*

There are different methods for anonymizing attribute data. These are intended for data dissemination (notably encouraged by the Open Data movement) by eliminating the risk of re-identification while maintaining data quality (Bergeat 2015). In the agricultural context, the Multipass project focuses on the protection of agricultural data in the context of their exchange with actors in the sector with the aim of transmitting only the bare minimum they need. It reports on four methods to guarantee the confidentiality of the information: the reduction of details that aims to go back to a broader level of detail (e.g. indicating the type of owner rather than their name), the addition of noise on the values that limit the possible links with other databases, the creation of a virtual dataset from the existing data for research purposes only and the encryption of the data using encryption methods (Croce et al. 2019; Pinet and Roussey 2020).

Aggregating data by classification leads to a form of anonymization by grouping entities with similar profiles into classes. It can be considered as a method of reducing details. Within the same class, individuals or entities present homogeneous characteristics on the whole but with a certain variability. This variability can notably be captured by the statistics characterizing the homogeneity of classes for each of the variables but eliminates the possibility of going back to the finer initial information.

3.2.2. *For localization*

Spatial aggregation by gridding is the most commonly used method for anonymizing information in a spatial context. Gridding is "a technique for cutting the territory into squares to disseminate statistical information at a low level of aggregation"[1]. INSEE, which aims on the one hand "to disseminate data with the highest possible level of usefulness" and on the other hand "to respect strong constraints of confidentiality of respondents", uses it for its statistical data (Buron and Fontaine 2018). This technique has many advantages, including freedom from any administrative zoning, ensuring "comparability between territories and over time" and making it possible to aggregate "to form custom study areas". While the gridding of statistical data ensures a certain level of confidentiality, it presents, according to Buron and Fontaine (2018), a risk of disclosure, that is, of deducing characteristics relating to an individual by cross-checking with other data (for example, statistical information at the scale of grid squares cross-checked with that of administrative units). This risk is increased in the case of low density. For a national statistical institute, methods are therefore used in addition to gridding to limit these risks with the disruption of microdata upstream and the addition of noise to cells downstream. On the other hand, the strategy for creating the grid is crucial in the anonymization process, especially with grid sizes that can be variable.

In our case, we do not have the precise locations of the farms (as we will see in the following) but an approximation by geometric approach. This location being de facto degraded, we will be satisfied with a grid without the additional precautions taken by an institute such as INSEE.

3.3. Data presentation: data in an agricultural context

For the analysis of agricultural areas in terms of spatial structure, land qualification and agri-environmental measures, we have the following sensitive data: the LPIS level 2, the Land files (Fichiers fonciers) and the AECM data. In addition, the computerized filiation documents (DFI), which are not sensitive, were used to study the evolution of the plots. Each piece of data is presented below according to its general characteristics (except for the LPIS, already described in Chapter 2), its sensitivity and, possibly, its imperfections.

---

1 Available at: https://www.insee.fr.

LPIS level2

The data in the LPIS is classified into three levels of dissemination. Level 1 or "anonymous", accessible to the general public for any reuse, does not contain the PACAGE identifiers that make it possible to identify the plots blocks belonging to the same farm. Then level 2 or "pseudonymized" (Pinet and Roussey 2020), accessible to the administrations referred to in article L 300-2 of the Public Administration Relations Code (CRPA), which contains the PACAGE identifier for each plots block. Finally, level 2+ or "non-anonymous", accessible only to state services, corresponds to the level 2 LPG to which is added a sheet containing all the personal elements of the farmer. For our analyses, we used the level 2 LPIS at three different dates (2009, 2016 and 2018) provided by the regional directorate of food, agriculture and forestry (DRAAF) in our four study territories. Regarding the rights of dissemination of these data integrating the PACAGE number, the General Regulation on Data Protection (RGPD) and articles L 311-5 and L 311-6 of the CRPA apply. This is information "whose communication would infringe on the protection of privacy [...] and commercial secrecy" (article L. 311-6 of the CRPA).

These data are subject to imperfections, particularly incompleteness. Indeed, as indicated in Chapter 2, the LPIS does not represent all of the agricultural land in a territory insofar as there are agricultural areas that do not give rise to a CAP declaration. For many reasons, the unrepresented agricultural plots may vary from one year to the next. For information, the difference between declared and real surfaces for the Pays de la Loire region is about 100,000 to 120,000 hectares[2]. This lack of completeness is further accentuated in our case by the fact that we only take into account the plots located within the limits of our study territories without taking into account the farms. Thus, only a subset of the declared plots of a farm is potentially taken into account. In addition, the LPIS does not contain any information that would allow one to discern the location of farms. It is also important to bear in mind the relative imprecision of the contours of the blocks and plots, which are drawn and can be modified by the farmer. Finally, in the context of diachronic studies, several problems may arise in relation to the evolution of the LPIS data. Thus, land use is provided at the plots block scale (defined as a set of contiguous crop plots declared by the same farm) for the period 2006–2014 and then at the crop plot level starting in 2015. Attribute data on

---

2 Information provided by DRAAF Pays de la Loire (2020).

land use increased from 28 crop groups before 2015 to over 300 crops starting in 2015. The farm numbers initially consisted of identifiers renewed each year and defined at the national level (2007–2009 period) and then at the departmental level (2010–2014 period) before acquiring stability over time because of the adoption of the PACAGE identifier in 2015, which poses problems for tracking farm plots over time. Despite these limitations, the LPIS is recognized as the most complete and therefore most relevant geographic database for addressing issues of spatial organization of agricultural plots (Preux et al. 2014).

Our analysis on the evolution of plot structure was based on plots blocks, the only relevant scale at the different dates considered (2009, 2015 and 2018), and our study on land typologies used blocks for the year 2009 and agricultural plots for 2016.

AECM

The AECM data give us information on the elements committed to agri-environmental and climatic measures. A committed element is an "element of the agricultural space upon which rests the agri-environmental and climatic obligations defined in the specifications of the agri-environmental and climatic measure subscribed"[3] by the farmer. They can have a surface modality (if the commitment concerns a group of plots or a grove), linear (if it concerns elements such as tree lines, hedges or ditches) or punctual (if it concerns, for example, isolated trees or ponds).

In our study area, these data are co-produced by the Agency for Services and Payment (ASP) and the Ministry of Agriculture and Food, on the one hand, and either the Pays de la Loire or Normandy regional council (depending on the area), on the other. Concerning the rights of diffusion, these data, which contain the PACAGE numbers, are subject to the same constraints and some of the same limitations as the LPIS level 2. For our analyses of farms, we used the AECM point, linear and surface data that are available only for the years 2015 and 2018 concerning the plots in our study area.

---

3 DRAAF, 2021. Technical Instruction on Agro-Environmental and Climate Measures (AECM) and aid for organic farming for the period 2015-2020. DGPE/SDPAC/2021-354 11/05/2021.

Other MAET (*Mesures Agro-Environnementales Territorialisées* or Territorialized agro-environmental measures) data, which provide us with information on the years of commitment localized at the plot level in the BVA between 2009 and 2013, were provided by the DDT (Departmental Directorate of Territories) of Maine-et-Loire. They have the same constraints and limitations as the LPIS level 2 (in particular, it is impossible to identify the plot of land of a farm). However, there are no restrictions concerning the identification of the year of the MAET. We have studied these data in the context of the analyses at the plot level.

Land files

The data known as "Land files" are delivered by the General Directorate of Planning, Housing and Nature (DGALN). They correspond to data from the application Update of Cadastral Data (MAJIC) of the General Directorate of Public Finances (DGFiP) reprocessed and enriched by the Center for Studies and Expertise on Risks, Environment, Mobility and Development (Cerema). They provide a detailed description of land, premises and the various property rights associated with them. In this sense, they are sensitive: their use requires a declaration to the CNIL and all measures must be taken by the user to "ensure the security of the information, and in particular to prevent it from being [...] communicated to unauthorized persons", this particular point concerning disclosure being covered by article 226-22 of the French Penal Code. For our analyses of the evolution profiles of agricultural plots, we mobilized the Land files at two different dates (2009 and 2015) for the communes of the BVA area.

These data are characterized by uncertainty in some columns such as "cgrnumd", which corresponds to the dominant crop group among the tax subdivisions and was used in our analyses. As indicated in the online documentation[4], this column has a rather poor degree of reliability (classified as "yellow") with "updating concerns" in its "finest modalities". It can nevertheless be used "thanks to groupings or special precautions". The data on the overall property typology ("typprop"), also used in our analyses, is more reliable (classified as "light green"), their only limitation being that

---

4 Online documentation for the parcel table in the Land files, version 2009: http://doc-datafoncier.cerema.fr/ff/doc_fftp/table/pnb10_parcelle/2009/.

"they may sometimes present discrepancies in relation to a field confrontation" due to the fact that they are based on declarative data. However, these discrepancies "may be considered insignificant on a municipal scale. The types of property most represented in the BVA are, for example, 'PERSON', 'COMMUNE' or 'PRIVATE CORPORATE PERSON'. The Land files also present imperfections on the geometries. First, there are gaps: for the year 2009, some plots were not vectorized, so their geometries are approximated by squares. Second, there are inaccuracies: for the same plot, the boundaries may be different from one year to the next. Thus, within the BVA perimeter, we note that the boundaries of theoretically identical plots in 2009 and 2016 diverge in the data (Figure 3.2) with shifts of up to 10 m. These may be plots that are documented as stable over time (case 1) or plots that have merged and whose overall boundary contours do not coincide on both dates (case 2).

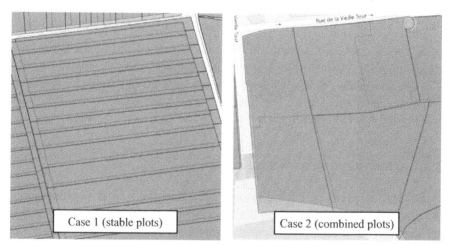

Figure 3.2. *Inconsistent parcel boundaries between 2009 (background layer) and 2016 (foreground layer with transparency) (openstreetmap background)*

DFI

The departmental files of computerized filiation documents (DFI) of plots provide information on "the plot modifications carried out since the computerization of their updating procedure, which, depending on the department, took place between the 1980s and the 1990s"[5]. They contain information on the origin (e.g. "survey documents" or "reorganization") and the date of the update. They are provided by the ministry in charge of the economy and finance, and are available in open data, so there are no confidentiality constraints.

Their main limitation is a lack of completeness: "changes resulting from rural land developments are not included because there is no geographic correspondence between the old and new plot names". For our analyses of the evolutionary patterns of agricultural plots, we used the DFIs with dates between January 1, 2009 and December 31, 2015, which concern the plots of the BVAs.

3.4. Treatments at the farm level: spatial structure versus AECM measures

In this section, we present the treatments carried out at the farm level, which aimed to characterize their spatial structures and the intensity of their AECM measures, which to some extent reflect the agri-environmental commitment of the farms. This analysis was carried out on the four study areas of the FARMaine project.

3.4.1. *Determining the virtual seats*

Several calculations of indicators describing the spatial organization of the plot of land require bringing the farm back to its center. Two possibilities are considered: a functional center corresponding to the farm headquarters and a geometric center corresponding to the barycenter (Puech et al. 2020). In the level 2 LPIS data, the location of the farm headquarters is not available. Thus, we consider the geometric center (also known as centroid, barycenter, or center of mass) of the farm's plots (Latruffe and Piet 2014; Figure 3.3). Taking into account the geometric center rather than the headquarters also allows us to reinforce the anonymization of the data, making re-identification of the farmer very difficult.

---

5 Available at: https://www.data.gouv.fr/en/datasets/documents-de-filiation-informatises-dfi-des-parcelles/.

In practice, the PACAGE number makes it possible to identify all the plots of land of the same farm. The centroid of the plots present in the sector can then be calculated for each farm. Each of these centroids thus corresponds to what we will call the "virtual seat" of a farm. The information on the structure and intensity of the AECM commitment of the farms, whose calculation methodology is presented below, is related to these points.

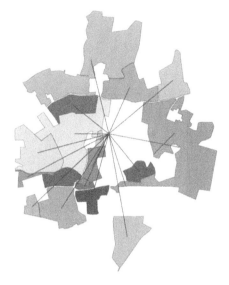

Figure 3.3. *Centroid of a farm: the polygons represent the blocks of a farm and the point corresponds to its centroid. For a color version of this figure, see www.iste.co.uk/pinet/geographic2.zip*

3.4.2. *Structure analysis: the indicators used*

Numerous methodological studies have focused on the study of the spatial structure of farms, particularly since Renard (1972), who proposed grouping and structure indices to measure plot fragmentation. The objective is generally to identify difficulties in farming conditions and to use them to evaluate economic and environmental performance (Puech et al. 2020).

There are two main types of indicators: fragmentation indicators, which aim to characterize the degree of division of the plot of land of a single farm into plots, and dispersion indicators, which characterize the distance and scattering between the plots of a single farm. Piet and Cariou (2013) identify several indicators of fragmentation: the number of plots per farm, the plot shape index, the average area of plots, the average distance of a block of plots from the farm's barycenter, the maximum distance of plots from the farm's barycenter, the average distance of a plot from its nearest neighbor and the share of the total farm area included in the equivalent area disk. These indicators can be combined. For example, Guittard et al. (2012) proposed a farm plot dispersion index that estimates the scattering of a farm's blocks of plots around the farm centroid, taking into account the size of the cluster.

Figure 3.4. *Principles of the fragmentation (left) and dispersion (right) indicators. For a color version of this figure, see www.iste.co.uk/pinet/geographic2.zip*

In this work, we constructed two indicators with the objective of simplifying implementation and based on the following principles (Figure 3.4). On the one hand, we consider that a farm has a high fragmentation index if it is characterized by a large number of plots blocks in relative value. On the other hand, we consider that the more a farm has a large number of plots blocks (in absolute value) and these clusters are far from its barycentre, the more this farm has a high dispersion index.

The fragmentation index corresponds to the number of plots blocks per farm in relation to a reference area of 100 hectares. Thus, the smaller the value, the less the farm is divided. This index does not take into account the shape of the plots blocks or their distance, but it remains interesting to approach the notion of division. It is calculated with the following formula:

$$\text{Fragmentation index} = \left(\frac{\text{Nb plots blocks}}{\text{Farming area}}\right) \times 100$$

For the calculation of the dispersion index, our method is based on the distance between the plots blocks and the center of the farm, on the one hand, and the number of plots blocks per farm, on the other hand. A first score from 1 to 4 was thus attributed to the farms according to their number of plots blocks and a second score (from 1 to 5) was attributed according to the cumulative distance between the center of the farm and all the centroids of the plots blocks. The dispersion index is the average of these scores (Figure 3.5).

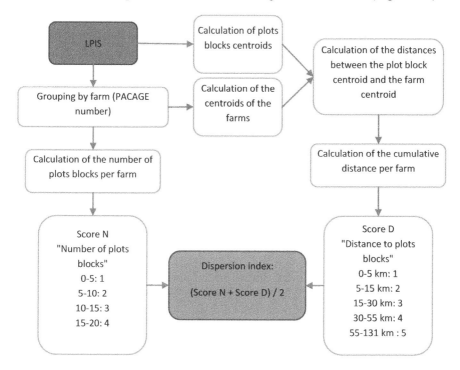

Figure 3.5. *Method of calculating the dispersion index*

3.4.3. *Analysis of AECM intensity*

For each farm and each year considered (2015 and 2018), three quantities were calculated: the numbers of specific AECMs, the cumulative lengths of linear AECMs, and the sums of the surface AECMs committed. These values were then normalized: for each quantity, they were divided by the maximum value observed in our data. These normalized values (i.e. between

0 and 1 inclusive) were then added together to obtain information reflecting the intensity of the commitment to AECM on the different farms.

3.4.4. *Introduction of uncertainty at the level of the location by squaring*

The structure and intensity indices of the AECM commitment were attached to the centroids of the farms. To further increase the uncertainty of this already degraded information (it appears complicated to be able to find the plots of a farm from its geometric center), we proceeded to a spatial aggregation by relating these data to squares.

In choosing the cell size, we considered that in the ideal case of a perfectly homogeneous distribution of farms in space, a grid cell should cover one farm. We therefore adopted as the cell size the average of the average areas of the farms on our perimeters in 2009, 2015 and 2018, that is, 435,600 m^2 or 660 m by 660 m. Of course, squares were created only at locations where "virtual seats" were located. Even if a square contains only one centroid, it is not possible to locate it precisely within that square, further limiting the possibility of re-identification.

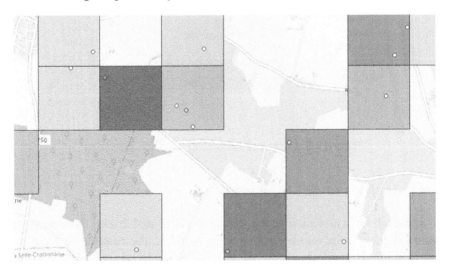

Figure 3.6. *Overlay of the operating centroids with the grid: the points and squares have a color code corresponding to the dispersion index (the darker the red the higher the dispersion) (openstreetmap background). For a color version of this figure, see www.iste.co.uk/pinet/geographic2.zip*

We then filled in each cell with the number of farm centroids it contains, the values (average in the case where there are several virtual seats in the cell) of the indices of dispersion, fragmentation and intensity of AECM measures of these farms. Then classes were defined to render these three indices in the form of categories (Figure 3.6).

It is thus possible to use these gridded data to obtain a cartographic view of the intensity of adoption of the AECMs or of the levels of dispersion and fragmentation of farms without revealing any IPI. These results are disseminated via the FarmSIG web platform in order to compare the evolution over time of the spatial structure and the intensity of adoption of AECM on farms. A 2D representation is interesting to appreciate the spatial distribution of each criterion taken individually (e.g. agri-environmental commitment or fragmentation in Figures 3.7 and 3.8) but is not well adapted to have an overall view of these criteria at a given year, and even more so for a multi-date approach.

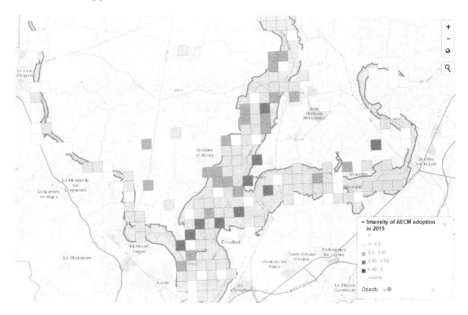

Figure 3.7. *Mapping the intensity of AECM adoption in 2015 in a BVA sector. For a color version of this figure, see www.iste.co.uk/pinet/geographic2.zip*

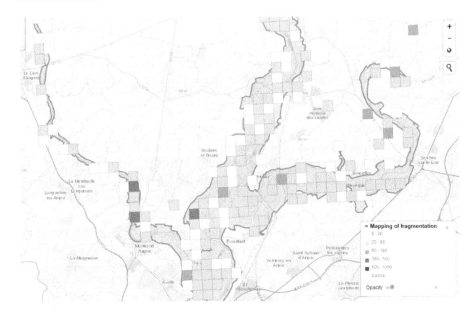

Figure 3.8. *Mapping of fragmentation in 2015 in one area of the BVA. For a color version of this figure, see www.iste.co.uk/pinet/geographic2.zip*

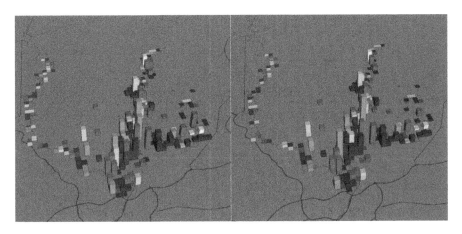

Figure 3.9. *AECM adoption intensity (height) versus fragmentation (color) in BVAs in 2015 (left) and 2018 (right). For a color version of this figure, see www.iste.co.uk/pinet/geographic2.zip*

A 3D rendering of the squares with a height that varies according to the degree of agri-environmental commitment and a color intensity relative to the level of fragmentation is presented in Figure 3.9, with a vertical division of the screen allowing one to compare two different years. It allows a better appreciation of the phenomena in all their dimensions. It can thus be seen that the farms near the Sarthe River have a significant and stable agri-environmental commitment over time and present a medium to pronounced fragmentation. The cartographic representations, constructed in either 2D or 3D, thus make it possible to read the general trends without the possibility of precisely identifying the farms and their characteristics.

3.5. Treatments at plot level: typology of land changes

In this section, we present the treatments carried out on the scale of agricultural plots in the BVA to build a multi-date database and then a typology of land changes between 2009 and 2016 according to the adoption of AECM.

3.5.1. *Construction of a multi-date database*

The constitution of the multi-date database took place in several steps with the objective of creating variables from the crossing of different databases. This crossing of databases to enrich the description of farms in different dimensions (properties, uses, land taxation) requires overcoming certain technical obstacles (ASP et al. 2015; de Rincquesen et al. 2016; Leger-Boch 2020) related in particular to the imprecision of the plot of land. In our case, new relevant variables must be chosen to address the temporal dimension, that is, the evolution of farms.

Initially, we kept only the plots comparable to the two years considered (2009 and 2016). Indeed, 2% of the BVA plots were not vectorized in 2009, their real geometries having been replaced by squares.

Then, after crossing the LPIS and the Land files, we calculated the majority agricultural occupation on each plot in 2009 and 2016. In order to avoid problems of relative inaccuracy of the contours between these two databases, a threshold of 20% is applied: an agricultural occupation must correspond to at least 20% of the surface of a plot to be retained. When it is not possible to deduce the agricultural occupation of the plots (intersection with the LPIS is too weak or non-existent), then the land occupation recorded in the Land files (column "cgrnumd" presented in section 3.3) is retained. Given the problem that this information may not be exact, we reduced the level of semantic detail to have a more general classification in three categories: "wooded plots" for the type 'WOODS', "miscellaneous agricultural plots" for the types 'MEADOWS', 'LANDS' or 'ORCHARDS', for example, and "non-agricultural plots" for the other values (such as 'GARDENS', 'LANDS' and 'SOIL'). The plots were also enriched with data on the year of commitment to AECM from the MAET data. We proceeded in the same way as with the land use from the LPIS.

In the third step, we cross-referenced the 2009 plot data with the 2016 plot data. As discussed in section 3.3, the plot geometries can have significant mismatches between the two years. A method based on the Space-Time Composite paradigm (Langran and Chrisman 1988) consisting of the intersection of all plots during the observation period is not applicable here because of these imperfections. We therefore performed a matching based on the DFI files that allowed us to reconstruct the parentage relationships between plots over the period 2009–2016. Three evolutions are thus observed on our territory: division, merging or stability of the plots (no complex evolution, such as recomposition, is observed).

We intersected the 2009 plot geometries with the 2016 ones in the case of mergers (96 plots). In the cases of division (216 plots) and stability (9459 plots), we kept the geometries of the 2016 plots. This allows us to keep both 2009 and 2016 information within the same geographical entities (9,771 in all), while ensuring the best possible topological consistency of the data (no overlaps between neighboring polygons).

In a fourth step, we calculated several descriptors concerning:

– the evolution of the plot based on the use of DFI files (variable named "evoparcelle" with the three modalities 'stability', 'reunion' or 'fusion');

– the evolution of the majority agricultural occupation on the plot according to the method described above (variable "ocs_evo") with modalities of the form "occupation in 2009-occupation in 2016" containing 79 different values, four of which are significant (greater than 5%) and reflect stabilities over time: "permanent grassland-permanent grassland" (36%), "miscellaneous agricultural plot-miscellaneous agricultural plot" (17.8%), "other plot-other plot" (16.3%) and "forest plot-forest plot" (11.2%);

– changes related to the owner of the plot of land based exclusively on the Land files (these are binary values: "change" or "no change"): change of owner if the communal account identifier has been modified ("evoprocpte"), change of owner type ("evotype_prop") and change of owner location ("evoloc_prop");

– the evolution of the type of exemption ("exo_evo") with modalities of the form "type of exemption in 2009–type of exemption in 2016", containing 18 different values, three of which are significant (greater than 5%): "TA-TA" for a maintenance of an exemption of the type "AGRICULTURAL LANDS" (53.5%), "TA-NA" for a change from an exemption of "AGRICULTURAL LANDS" to an exemption "NATURA 2000" (24.15%), "-" when there is no exemption over the period considered (12.5%) and "PB-PB" when there is a maintenance of an exemption for "WOODLAND PLANTATION" (5.2%);

– the year of the AECM commitment ("engagement_maet" between 2009 and 2013 inclusive).

3.5.2. *Classification*

We then performed a factorial analysis of these qualitative variables followed by a hierarchical ascending classification in order to identify farm evolution profiles in this territory. This typology based on evolution complements approaches based on land structuring (de Rincquesen et al. 2016) and more specifically on the ownership-use relationship (Léger-Bosch 2020) for a given date. The multiple correspondence analysis (MCA) carried out shows two trends in the data (Figure 3.10): the first factorial axis, which explains about 13.5% of their inertia, is related to the commitment to AECM, the evolution of the exemption and then the evolution of the agricultural land use. The second, which explains almost 12%, is related to a change in the landowner themself and their location. We note that the evolution of the plot plays no role. The second and third factorial axes (explaining more than 16% of the inertia of the data) underline the weight of the joint evolution of the exemption and of the agricultural land use in the observed evolution profiles.

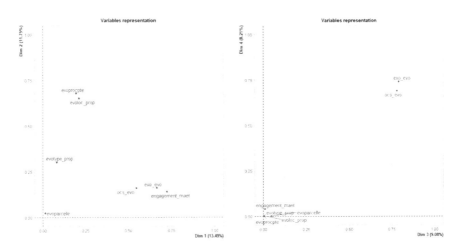

Figure 3.10. *Representation of the variables according to the factorial axes 1 and 2 (left) and 3 and 4 (right)*

A hierarchical ascending classification was carried out on 10 axes resulting from the MCA, which explain more than 75% of the variance of the data. It allows us to distinguish three main categories of land changes related to the adoption of AECM in our territory:

– the agricultural plots that were the subject of a commitment in AECM without change related to the owner, evolved toward a Natura 2000 exemption and remained permanent grasslands (2371 plots, i.e. 24.3% of the total);

– agricultural plots with no AECM commitment and no change in ownership that retained an agricultural land exemption (4839 plots, i.e. 49.5% of the total);

– the plots of land that have undergone a change of ownership have remained forested and continue to benefit from exemptions for the planting of woodland (2,561 plots, i.e. 26.2% of the total).

Thus, on the one hand, only the plots of land in the first category have experienced a dynamic towards agri-environmental commitments, and, on the other hand, only the plots of land in the third category have undergone a change of ownership.

3.5.3. *Measurement of uncertainty based on class homogeneity percentages*

The assignment of plots to categories introduces semantic uncertainties (within the same class, the profile is homogeneous but with a variability that can be quantified by class statistics) and therefore spatial uncertainties (a given plot is associated with a category but this does not allow us to know with certainty its evolution in terms of taxation and ownership) in our data.

Table 3.1 presents descriptive statistics for each class. In particular, we are interested in three values defined for each of the modalities: the share of plots with this modality that are in this class ("Cla/Mod"), the share of plots in the class with this modality ("Mod/Cla") and the share of plots with this modality in the whole data set ("Global"). The first value allows us to identify the modalities that discriminate between the different types and characterizes the probability for a plot with a given modality to be in a given class. The second value describes the homogeneity of the class for each of the modalities, allowing us to qualify the variability within a class. The third value is useful to relativize the first value by taking into account the weight of the modality in the data set. The table is broken down into three parts with different color codes corresponding to classes 1 (green), 2 (purple) and 3 (brown). In order to limit the risk of disclosure of sensitive information, we have coded the values: "f" (for low) corresponds to rates below 33%, "M" (for medium) to rates between 33% and 66% and "F" (for high) to rates greater than or equal to 66%. For example, we note that a large number of plots with a commitment in 2009 are in class 1 (column "Cla/Mod") and many plots in class 1 have a commitment to AECM dating from 2009 (column "Mod/Cla"), knowing that this type of commitment to AECM concerns a small proportion of the total number of plots (column "Global"). The more homogeneous the classes, the lower the intra-class variability and the greater the chance that a given plot has a given characteristic. For example, in class 1, a high proportion of the plots have a stable agricultural occupation profile of grassland type, that is, the possibility that a given plot in this class has this profile is high but not certain. Information at the plot level is disseminated via FarmSIG (Figure 3.11) with some uncertainty limiting the risk of knowing their evolution in terms of taxation, AECM commitment and ownership.

Modalities of the variables	Cla/Mod	Mod/Cla	Global
engagement_maet=2009	F	F	f
exo_evo=TA-NA	F	F	f
ocs_evo=Permanent grassland-Permanent grassland	M	F	M
engagement_maet=2013	F	f	f
engagement_maet=2012	F	f	f
evoloc_prop=NO CHANGE IN THE LOCATION OF THE OWNER	F	F	F
evotype_prop=NO CHANGE IN OWNERSHIP TYPE	F	F	F
evoprocpte=NO CHANGE OF OWNERSHIP	F	F	F
evoparcelle=STABLE PLOT	F	F	F
engagement_maet=NULL	M	F	F
exo_evo=TA-TA	F	F	M
evoloc_prop=NO CHANGE IN THE LOCATION OF THE OWNER	M	F	F
evoprocpte=NO CHANGE OF OWNERSHIP	F	F	F
evotype_prop=NO CHANGE IN OWNERSHIP TYPE	M	F	F
ocs_evo=miscellaneous agricultural plot-miscellaneous agricultural plot	F	f	f
ocs_evo=other plot-other plot	F	f	f
exo_evo=-	F	f	f
evoloc_prop=NULL	F	F	f
evoprocpte=CHANGE OF OWNER	F	F	f
evotype_prop=CHANGE OF OWNERSHIP TYPE	F	f	f
exo_evo=PB-PB	F	f	f
engagement_maet=NULL	M	F	F
ocs_evo= forest plot-forest plot	M	f	f
evoparcelle=DIVIDED PLOT	M	f	f
exo_evo=TA-TA	F	M	M

Table 3.1. *Statistics of the three categories of land evolution in relation to the agri-environmental commitment of agricultural plots in the BVA sector. For a color version of this table, see www.iste.co.uk/pinet/geographic2.zip*

Figure 3.11. *Map of the evolution of the plots on the FarmSIG site (openstreetmap background). For a color version of this figure, see www.iste.co.uk/pinet/geographic2.zip*

3.6. Conclusion and perspectives

We have proposed two distinct approaches to combine the presentation of analysis results related to the agricultural context in a readable and relevant form, via the FarmSIG website, while respecting confidentiality requirements. The first one consists of degrading, by a double process of centroid calculation and aggregation within a grid, the location of the farms in order to give an account of their spatial structures and their degrees of agro-environmental commitment. Two dissemination methods have been implemented: 2D and 3D (more advantageous for reporting complex phenomena). The second approach is based on the creation of a multi-date database used to produce a classification of land changes in plots in relation to their agro-environmental commitment between 2009 and 2016 in the BVAs. We showed that the classification process induced the introduction of semantic uncertainty that can be quantified. These analyses mobilized data whose imperfections had to be taken into account and their results meet the objectives by making it almost impossible to re-identify personal information.

With regard to the first analysis, other structural descriptors (such as those presented in section 3.4.2) could be calculated and disseminated, depending on their relevance, in order to provide additional keys to understanding the characteristics and evolution of farms in relation to the PEPs.

Concerning the second analysis, a more detailed study should include the variables used for classification: crop rotation, crop succession and farm dynamics (e.g. expansion and reduction). The LPIS Explorer tool could provide solutions for these issues (Levavasseur et al. 2016).

Regarding dissemination, the FarmSIG web-GIS still needs to be improved with the integration of 3D, temporal navigation tools or a more complete dashboard, especially for statistical results at the perimeter or class level. Particular care should be taken to make the user aware of the degraded and imprecise nature of the information displayed.

3.7. Acknowledgments

The authors thank Benjamin Balland and Rovasoa Voniarinjanahary for their contributions to this work through their graduate internships.

3.8. References

ASP, FNSAFER, SCAFR Terres d'Europe (2015). Rapport méthodologique relatif au croisement du Registre parcellaire graphique avec les fichiers du cadastre dans les 4 départements d'étude : Charente-Maritime, Mayenne, Nord, Oise. Report, MAAF, Programme 215, Marché SSP No. SSP-2013-090.

Bergeat, M. (2015). Anonymisation de données individuelles : bien calées, bien protégées ? *12èmes journées de méthodologie statistiques*, March 31–April 2.

Buron, M.-L. and Fontaine, M. (2018). Confidentialité des données spatiales. *Insee méthodes 131, Manuel d'analyse spatiale* [Online]. Available at: https://www.insee.fr/fr/information/3635442 [Accessed August 10, 2023].

Croce, L., Lemière, L., Bimonte, S., Pinet, F. (2019). Une nouvelle méthodologie pour l'anonymisation des entrepôts de données spatiales : application aux données de biodiversité dans le contexte agricole. *Revue des nouvelles technologies de l'information*, RNTI-B-15, 15–30.

Follin, J.-M., Girres, J.-F., Olteanu-Raimond, A.-M., Sheeren, D. (2019). The origins of imperfection in geographic data. In *Geographic Data Imperfection 1: From Theory to Applications*, Batton-Hubert, M., Desjardin, E., Pinet, F. (eds). ISTE Ltd, London, and John Wiley & Sons, New York.

Follin, J.-M., Voniarinjanahary, R., Thommeret, N., Fournier, M. (2021). FarmSIG : une application web pour l'analyse de l'évolution des espaces agricoles en lien avec les politiques publiques environnementales. *16th Spatial Analysis and GEOmatics Conference SAGEO'2021 – La Rochelle*, May 5–7.

Fournier, M. (2016). FARMaine, Foncier, Aménagement et Régulations dans le bassin de la Maine. Projet PSDR 4, Grand Ouest, Série Les 4 pages PSDR4.

Langran, G. and Chrisman, N.R. (1988). A framework for temporal geographic information. *Cartographica: The International Journal for Geographic Information and Geovisualization*. 25(3), 1–14.

Latruffe, L. and Piet, L. (2014). Does land fragmentation affect farm performance? A case study from Brittany, France. *Agricultural Systems*, 129, 68–80.

Léger-Bosch, C. (2020). Qui possède et qui utilise les terres agricoles ? Vers une lecture territoriale de l'intersection des données de la fiscalité foncière française (Majic) et de la politique agricole commune (RPG). *Symposium PSDR4. Transitions pour le développement des territoires. Connaissances et pratiques innovantes pour des modèles agricoles, alimentaires et forestiers résilients*, Angers, October 28–30.

Levavasseur, F., Martin, P., Bouty, C., Barbottin, A., Bretagnolle, V., Thérond, O., Scheurer, O., Piskiewicz, N. (2016). RPG explorer: A new tool to ease the analysis of agricultural landscape dynamics with the Land Parcel Identification System. *Computers and Electronics in Agriculture*, 127, 541–552.

Piet, L. and Cariou, S. (2014). Le morcellement des exploitations agricoles françaises. *Économie rurale* [Online]. Available at: http://journals.openedition. org/economierurale/4408 [Accessed September 27, 2021].

Pinet, F. and Roussey, C. (2020). Multipass. Episode "L'anonymisation des données" [Online]. Available at: https://numerique.acta.asso.fr/multipass3 anonymisation/.

Preux, T., Delahaye, D., Marie, M. (2014). Intérêts et limites de l'usage du registre parcellaire graphique pour l'étude du processus d'agrandissement des exploitations agricoles. Exemple de la mise en place d'un suivi à haute fréquence en Basse-Normandie. *Conference Proceedings "Le foncier agricole : usages, tensions, régulations"*. SFER- ENS Lyon.

Puech, T., Durpoix, A., Barataud, F., Mignolet, C. (2020). Une méthode pour caractériser l'organisation spatiale des parcellaires d'exploitations agricoles. *Cybergeo: European Journal of Geography*, document 938 [Online]. Available at: https://journals.openedition.org/cybergeo/34181 [Accessed August 10, 2023].

Renard, J. (1972). Recherches méthodologiques sur le degré d'émiettement parcellaire des exploitations agricoles des bocages de l'ouest. *Bulletin de l'Association de géographes français*, 49(397), 83–94.

de Rincquesen, H., Julien, V., Lécuyer, C., Levesque, R., Liorit, D., Melin, M., Pathier, G., Quelin, C. (2016). Appariement entre le registre parcellaire graphique et le cadastre pour construire une typologie des exploitations françaises. *NESE*, 41, 51–82.

The Representation of Uncertainty Applied to Natural Risk Management

4.1. Introduction

In recent years, the frequency of natural disasters (cyclones, floods, etc.) has increased considerably around the world. Faced with these destructive phenomena, populations and institutions must be prepared to reduce their vulnerability to possible damage by developing skills at all stages of natural risk management.

Natural risk management uses geographic information and associated cartographic representations, both after a natural disaster (to map the hazards and their damage, and to plan reconstruction) and before a disaster (in particular to warn the population and prepare for possible evacuations). In this chapter, we will only be interested in cartographic documents, elaborated before natural disasters in hazard prevention logic.

The main difficulty encountered in the elaboration of a natural hazard prevention plan is the uncertainty associated with the delimitation of the zones impacted by a potential natural hazard. Indeed, natural hazards are by definition uncertain phenomena, both in their spatial dimension (extent of direct and indirect impacts) and temporal dimension (duration and frequency of the catastrophic event). Thus, taking into account the uncertainty associated with the delimitation of danger zones is an integral part of the representation of natural hazards, and we intend to study it here.

Chapter written by Jean-François GIRRES.

This chapter therefore aims to analyze how uncertainty is taken into account in the delimitation of hazard areas associated with natural hazards, and how it is represented in cartographic documents. For this purpose, this study will be based on the analysis of risk prevention plans associated with three natural hazards (marine submersion, flooding and avalanches).

The study of risk prevention plans in France shows that the uncertainty associated with natural hazards is mainly related to the intensity of the hazard (especially water heights), and to a lesser extent, the history of hazards (especially for avalanches). From a cartographic point of view, a semiological analysis of the legends used in different natural hazard prevention plans shows that the uncertainty associated with the intensity of the hazard is mainly shown by the use of color gradients. This analysis also shows that the original methods of uncertainty representation developed in recent years in the field of geovisualization research are not used at the operational level to represent the uncertainty associated with natural hazards.

In the first section, this chapter will review the notion of natural hazards and the associated uncertainty. In the second section, a state of the art on the methods of uncertainty representation will be presented by relating the interest of their use to decision-making processes. Then, an analysis of the representation of uncertainty in natural hazard prevention plans in France will be proposed. Finally, original contributions of uncertainty representation will be presented by evoking their interest in the field of natural risk management.

4.2. Natural hazards: uncertain phenomena

Natural hazards are phenomena characterized by a high degree of uncertainty. A reminder of the fundamental concepts associated with the notion of natural hazards will allow us to better understand the sources of spatiotemporal uncertainties that govern their modeling.

4.2.1. *Risk, hazard and exposure*

It is commonly accepted in the scientific community that natural hazards result from the intersection between the probability that a destructive natural phenomenon will occur, and the possible damage that this phenomenon may cause to property and people located in a given area [JON 01, UND 04]. The risk can be formulated by equation [4.1]:

$$R = H * (E * V)$$ [4.1]

where: R = Risk

H = Hazard

E = Exposure

V = Vulnerability

The hazard covers both the potentially destructive natural phenomena (earthquake, flood, etc.) as well as the probabilistic expression of this potential (e.g. the frequency and magnitude of a flood at a given location). The exposure corresponds to the properties and people exposed directly or indirectly to the hazards. These stakes are characterized by a vulnerability, which reflects their fragility in the face of a hazard, but also their ability to restore themselves after damage (i.e. their resilience). It is important to note at this level that there is no risk, strictly speaking, without stakes to protect. These stakes can be human, material, but also natural (an ecological heritage), or even landscape.

From a terminological point of view, it is important to distinguish risk management from crisis management. Traditionally, risk management is considered to be a preventive approach that uses tools, methods and actions that take place before disasters occur. Crisis management intervenes at the time of a disaster by ensuring the safety of people and property, and after the disaster by restoring "normal" conditions and rebuilding after damage.

Nevertheless, risk management can be considered as a global approach, which integrates both the prevention phase, but also the crisis management and reconstruction phases (post-crisis phase). In this chapter, we will focus on the first approach, where risk management is approached in its prevention phase.

To formalize the methodological approach to natural risk management, the hazard management continuum formalism can be used. This formalism integrates the different risk-management phases in a systemic and rational way. As illustrated in Figure 4.1, the reconstruction phase (or post-crisis phase) can be considered as a loop with the crisis prevention and preparation phase, through the enrichment of a collective memory on the hazard and its consequences, allowing us to reduce the vulnerability of exposed populations as well as the associated risk.

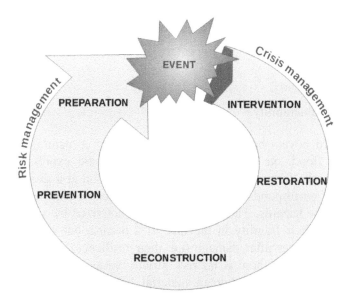

Figure 4.1. *The risk management cycle [FOC 01]*

Within the framework of this book, we will focus on the prevention and preparation phases. This will be done through the development of cartographic documents or geo-visualization tools designed to prevent populations and stakes exposed to natural hazards.

4.2.2. *Spatial and temporal uncertainty of natural hazards*

Natural hazards are by definition uncertain phenomena. From an etymological point of view, the term *hazard* refers to a random phenomenon, that is, an unpredictable event.

Natural hazards are defined by the combination of a magnitude (i.e. its power), a probability of occurrence, an area of impact and a duration of action. However, it is impossible to predict with certainty the occurrence, spatial extent, or magnitude of a natural hazard. If the occurrence of some meteorological hazards is more or less predictable on a seasonal basis in some geographical areas (such as hurricanes in the Gulf of Mexico, or Mediterranean phenomena in the south of France for example), it is impossible to predict with accuracy their spatial extension or their magnitude.

Moreover, the different types of natural hazards are subject to both spatial (in terms of the spatial extension of the disaster) and temporal (in terms of the duration of the phenomenon, and its frequency) variability. Figure 4.2 represents the spectrum of natural hazards on a graph showing the spatial extension of a hazard in relation to its duration [LEO 10].

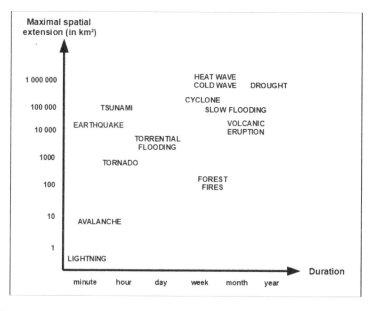

Figure 4.2. *Spatiotemporal classification of hazards according to [LEO 10]*

4.2.3. *Sources of uncertainty in natural hazard modeling*

In a logic of natural risk management, maps representing the potential impact of a natural hazard are produced in order to prevent and prepare the exposed populations. These maps are based on a modeling of natural hazards, whose main objective is to define a probable spatial extension. As such, the definition of the spatial extension of natural hazards is subject to uncertainty, which can be caused by different issues:

– the variation of the probable intensity of the hazard;

– the imperfection of the data used to model the hazard;

– the methods used to model the extension of the hazard.

For example, to model a marine flooding phenomenon, the hazard area may vary according to different criteria:

– the expected water level;

– the digital terrain model used;

– the attenuation of water height based on inland penetration.

Using the process approach proposed by Barsalou [BAR 14] and adapted to the imperfection of geographic data in [FOL 19], Figure 4.3 illustrates the different components of uncertainty associated with the delineation of hazard areas for marine submersion hazard mapping.

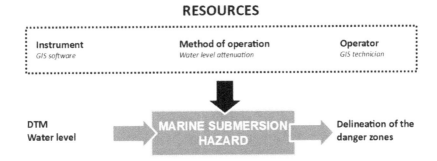

Figure 4.3. *Uncertainty components of hazard zone delineation in the face of marine submersion hazard. For a color version of this figure, see www.iste.co.uk/pinet/geographic2.zip*

From these three causes of uncertainty, the delineation of the marine submersion hazard may vary greatly. This is illustrated in Figure 4.4, through the delineation of marine submersion hazard areas in Martinique, using:

– projected water heights (without attenuation) of 2, 5 and 10 m (a);

– a projected water height (without attenuation) of 10 m on BDALTI and SRTM altimetry data (b);

– a water level of 10 m on BDALTI without attenuation, or with an attenuation of 1 m for every 200 m of land penetration (c).

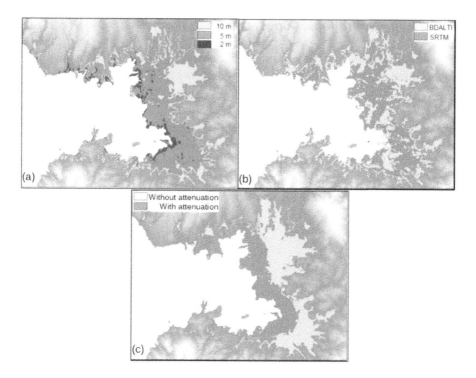

Figure 4.4. *Marine submersion areas modeled with different water heights (a), altimetry data (b) and attenuation methods (c). For a color version of this figure, see www.iste.co.uk/pinet/geographic2.zip*

This simple example illustrates the difficulty in defining the spatial extension of hazards with uncertain characteristics. This raises questions about the existing methods of representing spatial uncertainty and their adaptability in the field of risk prevention.

4.3. Spatial representation of uncertainty: methods and interpretation

Different methods can be used to model and represent uncertain spatial phenomena. These representation methods will be associated with the general principles of graphic semiology, which governs the use of graphic signs in cartography. To conclude, we will question the interest of certain methods for representing uncertainty in the context of decision-making associated with natural risk management.

4.3.1. *Representation of uncertain spatial objects*

The representation of uncertain spatial objects was addressed in [BAT 19] through the concepts of broad boundary objects and fuzzy spatial objects.

Objects with broad boundaries are "vague" regions [PIN 10]. The question of their representation is introduced by the theory of the egg yolk [COH 96], which defines a vague boundary by means of an interior region of the object (the "yolk") considered as certain, and an exterior region (the "white") whose boundary is uncertain. These two regions are adjacent, and their union composes the "egg".

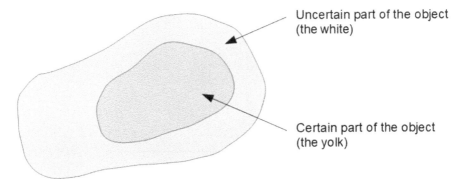

Figure 4.5. *The egg yolk model used to delineate vague spatial objects.*
For a color version of this figure, see www.iste.co.uk/pinet/geographic2.zip

The egg yolk theory thus differentiates in a discrete way a part considered as certain, and a part considered as uncertain. These two parts will be represented graphically in a different way.

Fuzzy objects, derived from the theory of fuzzy sets of [ZAD 76], allow to quantify a point's degree of membership to a spatial object by means of a membership function. Any point in space is thus defined by a degree of membership in the interval [0, 1]. A value of 1 means that the point belongs to the region for sure, while a value of 0 means that the object does not belong to the region.

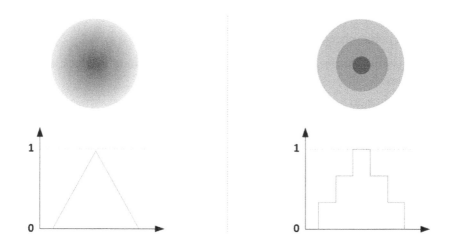

Figure 4.6. *Continuous (left) and discrete (right) representation of fuzzy objects.
For a color version of this figure, see www.iste.co.uk/pinet/geographic2.zip*

To represent a point's degree of belonging to a region, the use of a "gradient" allows us to continuously represent the uncertainty associated with the fuzzy object. As presented in [BAT 19], the use of alpha-cuts can also be mobilized in order to obtain a discrete representation of the fuzzy spatial object (Figure 4.6).

4.3.2. *Visual variables for representing uncertainty*

In order to formalize the methods for representing uncertainty graphically, the visual variables proposed by Bertin [BER 67] are used. The use of graphic signs in a map is governed by rules of graphic semiology, which allow the map's symbolism to be adapted according to the type of information being represented, and the reader's capacity for visual perception.

The rules of graphic semiology in cartography were mainly formalized by the work of Bertin [BER 67], who proposes to use the following seven visual variables to represent qualitative and quantitative phenomena in a map (Figure 4.7):

– the form: change of the external structure of a punctual or linear figure;

– the size: change of the surface of a point or linear figure;

– the color: change of the shade of a figure;

– the value: variation of the ratio between the quantity of black and white of a figure;

– the texture: change of the internal structure of a surface figure;

– the grain: variation of the size of a screen of surface figure by preserving the same ratio black/white;

– the orientation: variation of the angle of a figure.

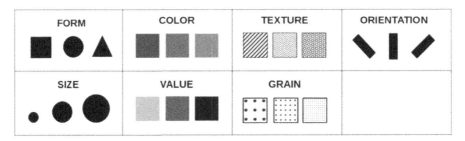

Figure 4.7. *The seven visual variables proposed by Bertin [BER 67]. For a color version of this figure, see www.iste.co.uk/pinet/geographic2.zip*

Each of the visual variables allows for the translation of a relation between the represented data, which can be a relation of difference, similarity, order or quantity. Thus, from a purely theoretical point of view, the representation of the different degrees of uncertainty refers to an order relation in the data, which can be represented by the visual variables "size", "value" or "grain". As we shall see, in practice, it is mainly the visual variable "value" that is used.

As such, the methods for representing uncertainty (for vague or fuzzy spatial objects) introduced in the previous section mainly refer to a use of the visual variable "value" to indicate the degree to which a point belongs to a region.

Thus, the representation of vague spatial objects with a broad boundary mainly involves a variation in value, with a higher intensity in the so-called "certain" regions and a lower intensity in the so-called "uncertain" regions. We will see later that the visual variable "color" can also be used to differentiate (and not scale) regions of certainty from regions of uncertainty. The representation of fuzzy objects also mobilizes a continuous value variation by using a membership function, while the use of alpha-cuts is based on a discrete value variation for each uncertainty class.

4.3.3. *Representation of uncertainty and decision-making*

Cartographic documents remain as decision support tools, and this is particularly the case in the field of natural hazard prevention, since the safety of goods and people depends on them. It is therefore fundamental that the symbolism used in the chart allows for the transmission of clear and appropriate information to the reader. This raises questions about the capacity of the methods of representing uncertainty proposed above to facilitate decision making.

Numerous authors have addressed issues related to the decision-making process with imperfect or uncertain geographic data, particularly in the field of natural hazards [TAC 09]. However, few works have really focused on the impact of the representation of uncertainty on the decision-making process. Among these works, we can notably mention the empirical study conducted by Hope and Hunter [HOP 06].

In this research, the authors compared the decision making of a sample of users based on several representations of danger zones with uncertain boundaries. The test persons had to change the direction of a boat (initially located in a zone marked A) before it arrived in a danger zone (marked B) with uncertain boundaries. Several representations of uncertain boundaries were proposed (Figure 4.8): a single line boundary (a), a multi-line boundary indicating probable entry into a hazard zone (b) and a continuous gradient (c).

The results of the test show that the way in which the uncertainty is represented in Area B has a strong influence on the users' decision making.

Thus, this study concluded that when boundaries are clearly determined by a line, users are quicker to reach safety. In contrast, when a boundary was not clearly represented (e.g. in the case of a gradient), users were more likely to continue into the danger zone [HOP 06].

The results of this study tend to show that the use of continuous gradients to represent hazard zones can be counterproductive in operational applications, since in the absence of clear boundaries of the hazard zones, users can take additional risks. A more suitable alternative is to represent the hazard in a discrete gradient, corresponding to several levels of alpha-cuts. It allows us to visually combine the intensity of the danger (by a gradient), with well-identified danger levels, visually separated by lines.

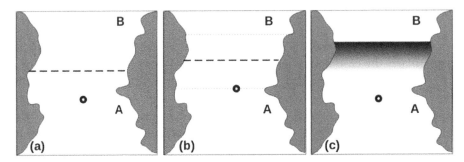

Figure 4.8. *Examples of uncertain boundary representations between a safety zone (denoted A) and a danger zone (denoted B) [HOP 06]*

Thus, in the following section, we will be interested in analyzing the different uncertainty representation methods used in operational cartographic documents, namely natural hazard prevention plans.

4.4. Analysis of uncertainty in natural hazard prevention maps

The objective of this section is to study how the uncertainty in the delimitation of hazard zones is taken into account in the cartographic documents of natural hazard prevention. For this purpose, the Natural Risk Prevention Plans (PPRNs) will be analyzed in order to study the rules of graphic semiology used to represent hazard zones and the associated uncertainty in their delimitation.

4.4.1. *Risk prevention plans*

The PPRNs were created by the law of February 2, 1995. Today, they are one of the essential instruments of the state's action in terms of natural risk prevention, with the aim of reducing the vulnerability of people and property. The objective of the PPRNs is to delimit the zones exposed directly or indirectly to a natural hazard and to regulate land use. This regulation can go as far as prohibiting construction.

The PPRNs take into account different natural hazards, such as floods for example, but also earthquakes, land movements, forest fires and avalanches.

A PPRNs file contains the following elements:

– a note presenting the context and the procedure carried out (reasons for the prescription of the PPR, known hazard, stakes, etc.);

– one or several cartographic documents describing the considered hazards and the regulatory zoning;

– a regulation corresponding to this zoning (prohibition or prescription, measures of protection, prevention or safeguard).

Here, we will focus only on mapping documents that delineate hazard zones associated with different natural hazards, and more specifically on hazard maps (as illustrated in Figure 4.9).

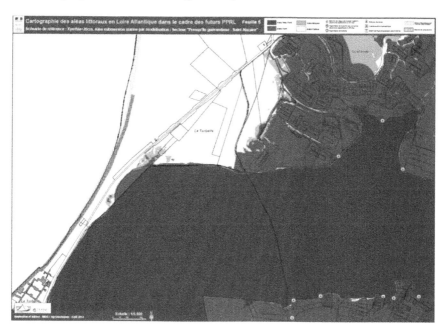

Figure 4.9. *Risk prevention plan for marine submersion in Loire-Atlantique. Guérande – Saint-Nazaire sector [PRE 14]. For a color version of this figure, see www.iste.co.uk/pinet/geographic2.zip*

4.4.2. *Modeling of hazard zones in risk prevention plans*

The hazard map is used to delimit the ground area of a rare catastrophic natural phenomenon (centennial or higher). In the case of floods, the hazard map is used to classify the heights of water likely to submerge the land. It is not a regulatory document, but a document of knowledge allowing the construction of the regulatory zoning plan. This hazard mapping is based on historical elements as well as on modeling, and varies according to the hazards considered. We will focus here on the hazards of marine submersion, flooding and avalanches.

The estimation of the marine submersion hazard is based on the intersection between the topography of coastal areas (modeled in France with the LITTO3D database) and a reference sea level. This reference sea level corresponds to a 100-year level, to which we add the impact of climate change (by an increase of 20 cm).

The reference sea levels are then projected on the digital terrain model, which allows us to define hazard zones corresponding to different water heights (e.g. 50 cm, 1 m and 2 m). In addition to these hazard zones, local surveys are carried out in order to determine the flow velocity of the water. The combination of water height and flow velocity allows the identification of different hazard levels. For example, in the Bay of Saint-Brieuc's PPR, the "very strong" hazard corresponds to water heights greater than 2 m (regardless of the flow velocity), or to water heights between 1 and 2 m, with a flow velocity greater than 0.5 m/s.

In the case of floods, it is mainly the height of the water that is taken into account in the delimitation of hazard zones. The water height is determined in relation to a reference level, such as a 100-year flood. Thus, in the municipality of Anduze's (Gard) PPR, the "strong" hazard corresponds to water heights of more than 50 cm above the reference level, and the "moderate" level corresponds to water heights of less than 50 cm. In some PPRs, such as that of Amiens, hazard zones are obtained by crossing the water height and the duration of submergence. Thus, the "strong" hazard corresponds here to water heights greater than 1 m (regardless of the duration of submergence) or to water heights between 0.5 m and 1 m, for a period greater than 2.5 m.

Finally, in the case of an avalanche, the definition of the hazard zone is generated from a reference event. The reference hazard is determined from its probability of occurrence and its intensity, which corresponds to a frequency of the order of 100 years. Avalanches are mainly characterized by two components: their intensity and their expansion. The intensity is defined mainly by the impact pressure exerted on a given point, thus translating its destructive power. The extension represents the area likely to be reached by the phenomenon of reference in its zone of departure, transit and arrival. The definition of the hazard zones is therefore done by crossing these two components.

4.4.3. Methodology for analyzing the representation of uncertainty

To carry out the analysis of the methods of representing uncertainty in risk prevention plans, a sample of 46 risk prevention plans located on the whole French territory was used [SOL 16].

Figure 4.10. Location of PPRs used in the analysis [SOL 16]. For a color version of this figure, see www.iste.co.uk/pinet/geographic2.zip

These 46 risk prevention plans are distributed as follows according to the natural hazards considered:

– 15 flood hazard maps;

– 17 marine submersion hazard maps;

– 14 avalanche hazard maps.

The main problem encountered in carrying out this analysis is the availability of maps. The prefectural websites often provide risk prevention plans and regulatory zoning documents, but do not always provide hazard maps.

A grid was created to analyze the representation of hazard zones, identifying the number of classes defined, their names and their representations. This study makes it possible to list the methods of representing uncertainty related to the spatial delimitation of the hazard [SOL 16, GIR 17].

4.4.4. *Results and comments*

The representation of uncertainty in hazard map delineation of risk prevention plans focuses on the uncertainty associated with the intensity of the hazard. In this section, we will present the number of intensity classes, the naming and the visual variable used. Finally, we will see that other forms of representation of uncertainty, notably in avalanche maps, are proposed in some hazard maps.

The analysis of hazard intensity classes is detailed in Table 4.1, which presents the number of classes in the different marine submersion, avalanche and flood hazard maps.

	2 Classes	3 Classes	4 Classes	5 Classes	Total
Marine submersion	2	2	13	0	17
Flooding	1	8	6	0	15
Avalanches	1	5	2	6	14
Total	6	15	21	6	

Table 4.1. *Number of hazard intensity classes in the marine submersion, avalanche and flood PPRs*

In the vast majority of marine submersion hazard maps (13 out of 17), four hazard classes are presented. The denomination used is more or less the same on all of the maps. In particular, the "strong" hazard is found on all maps, regardless of the number of classes. For the four class maps, we regularly find the "weak", "medium/moderate" and "strong" hazard classes. Variations are observed on the extreme classes, such as "very high hazard" and sometimes "very low hazard". About half of the flood hazard maps have three hazard classes (8 out of 15), and the hazard is generally divided into "low", "medium", "high" or "moderate", "high", "very high". On six maps, the flood hazard is divided into four hazard areas and a single map identifies only two hazard classes ("moderate" and "strong").

In contrast to the marine submersion and flood maps, avalanche maps are mostly multi-hazard maps. The hazard zones are still identifiable according to color codes and the different hazards are represented by letters ("A" for avalanche, "P" for rock fall, "G" for landslide). Of the 14 maps studied, six of them present five hazard classes: "negligible", "weak", "medium", "strong" and "very strong", with an additional class which is the "maximum likelihood hazard" (MLH) or "exceptional hazard zone". The area covered by the MLH is an "area affected by an exceptional event, higher than the 100-year level". This is a phenomenon that occurs most often in avalanche flood situations. The number of avalanche hazard classes varies greatly: five maps show three hazard classes, two maps show four classes and one map shows only two classes.

These results show first of all that the uncertainty associated with the intensity of the hazard is represented in a very variable manner, and that there is no real consensus on the definition of the number of classes. In the sample studied, the subdivision into four intensity classes remains the most used (21 maps out of 46). Moreover, if the "strong" hazard is regularly used in the naming of hazard classes, a semantic vagueness remains between "medium" or "moderate" hazards.

The second point analyzed concerns the representation of hazard classes, using different visual variables. Table 4.2 presents the visual variables used to scale and differentiate the hazard intensity classes in the marine submersion, flooding and avalanche PPRs.

	Value	Color	Combination	Grain	Total
Marine Submersion	6	8	3	0	17
Flooding	6	7	2	0	15
Avalanches	4	6	3	1	14
Total	16	21	8	1	

Table 4.2. *Visual variables used to represent hazard intensity classes*

For the marine submersion maps, three visual variables are used. First, the visual variable of color is used for slightly less than half of the maps (eight maps), as well as the use of value (for six maps), and finally a combination of texture and color for three maps. For some maps, an inappropriate use of visual variables is observed, especially the visual variable of color. Indeed, as mentioned by Bertin, it is not advisable to use several colors of the visible spectrum to represent ordered data with a single progression [CHE 04]. However, the classification of hazard areas according to their intensity constitutes ordered and graduated data. The use of the visual variable of value is therefore theoretically preferred. On some maps, the hazard areas are represented by associating the color to the texture, without there being any links between the different areas. In this case, the hazard levels are represented in a dissociative (and unordered) way.

The main problem with avalanche maps, which are multi-hazard maps, is their readability. The hazard zones are well defined, but the identification of the associated hazard remains complicated. Indeed, some areas are affected by not only avalanches but also landslides and rock falls. The different hazards are identified by a letter and a number that represents the degree of hazard. This abundance of information is therefore detrimental to the general readability of the document. As with the marine submersion maps, color is the most used visual variable (six maps), ahead of the use of value (four maps) and the combination of color and texture (three maps). Only one map uses grain. However, it can be seen that the colors used are similar for the representation of the different levels of hazards. This similarity in the choice of representation colors is explained by the fact that the majority of the hazard maps were produced by the "Restoration of Mountain Land" department of the National Forestry Office (ONF). This representation was then used in other municipalities, which explains this homogeneity.

Finally, on the flood maps, the visual variable of value is used more than for the other two hazards (six of 15 maps). Color is still used quite a bit (seven maps) and the combination of texture and color is used on two maps. In most of the flood maps where color is used, it is not used in an adapted way. Indeed, most maps use two color ranges (e.g. yellow-green-blue and yellow-orange-red), whereas for representing ordered data, the use of one range is recommended. Unlike the marine flooding and avalanche maps, some flood maps represent a class of uncertainty. This is notably the case for the commune of Nîmes, where the residual hazard class is represented where "the limit of the moderate hazard is uncertain".

The results of this analysis of visual variables used for representing hazard intensity classes also show that the representation rules suffer from a lack of homogeneity. It is also apparent that visual variables are often not used effectively. Indeed, to represent ordered hazard classes, the visual variable of color (with dissociative capacities) is generally preferred to the visual variable of value (with order capacities).

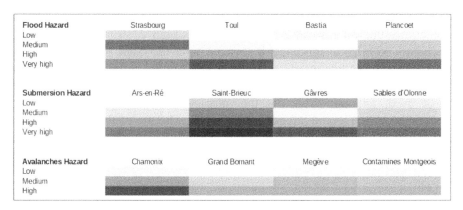

Figure 4.11. *Example of legends used in different PPRs. For a color version of this figure, see www.iste.co.uk/pinet/geographic2.zip*

Figure 4.11 provides an overview of the variety of colors used to represent hazard intensity classes in different PPRs. However, a harmonization of legends for avalanche hazards can be observed, essentially linked to the standardized practices of the main cartographic author (in this case the ONF).

4.5. Representation of uncertainty in risk maps: assessment and perspectives

This last section summarizes the current methods of uncertainty representation in risk maps, and more particularly in hazard maps of risk prevention plans. As a perspective, original contributions of the representation of uncertainty resulting from geovisualization research will be presented, in order to consider new forms of uncertainty representation in maps related to natural risk management.

4.5.1. *How uncertain are risk prevention plans?*

From the sample of the maps analyzed, it can be stated that there are no common rules in the definition and representation of hazard areas in the hazard maps of risk prevention plans, be it in terms of the number of classes, their definition and naming, or the symbology used. The uncertainty in the delimitation of the danger zones here relates only to the level of intensity of the hazard, whose classification is associated with a semantic which is sometimes unclear ("weak", "moderate", "medium", "strong" hazard). It is necessary to refer to the notes associated with the maps to understand the meaning of these classes (in terms of water heights, duration or speed, for example). As far as the visual variable is concerned, it is color that is the most used, although it is not the most adapted to represent graduated phenomena, such as the intensity of a hazard. The use of the visual variable of value should in theory be preferred, but in practice, color is often preferred, because of the strong symbolic significance of certain colors (green, yellow, red).

In addition, out of all of the hazard maps, only two maps represent an uncertain hazard class on the cartographic document. This zone of uncertainty is the "residual hazard" class (represented in light gray) on the flooding PPR of the municipality of Nîmes (see Figure 4.12). This zone is defined here in the PPRI presentation report "if the hazard is diffuse, or the limit of the moderate hazard is uncertain". The other maps do not mention the presence of uncertainty on the cartographic document. It is only mentioned in the presentation notes accompanying the maps, or because the methodologies for the realization of risk prevention plans stipulate that a margin of uncertainty must be taken into account.

Figure 4.12. *Residual hazard zones (in gray) on the Flood PPR of Nîmes [PRE 12].*
For a color version of this figure, see www.iste.co.uk/pinet/geographic2.zip

The only formal representations of uncertainty have been found in the Probable Avalanche Location Maps (CLPA), set up by INRAE (ex-CEMAGREF and ex-IRSTEA) and the Ministry of Ecological Transition (ex-Ministry of Ecology, Sustainable Development, and Energy) [BOR 94]. These are "descriptive maps of observed or historical phenomena". They represent both the results of studies made from photo-interpretation and field analysis (orange) and a collection of testimony by survey (purple), as shown in Figure 4.13.

The legend differentiates between avalanche areas whose boundaries are known and identified (shown with a solid fill and a thick border), avalanche zones "whose points are exposed to avalanches of varying magnitude" (with solid hatching and a thinner border), and finally, presumed avalanche zones for which there is a lack of precise information (dotted lines for the filling and the border of these zones). The uncertainty of the avalanche zones is thus clearly presented by this variation in filling and boundaries, differentiating between the delineation method used (photo-interpretation and field analysis, versus testimony).

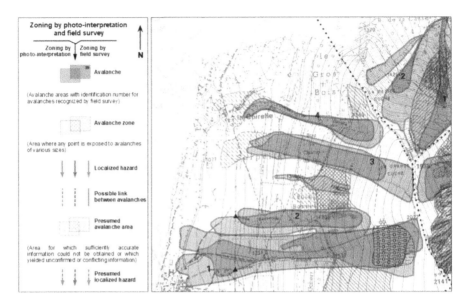

Figure 4.13. *Symbology used for avalanche occurrence maps [INR 05].*
For a color version of this figure, see www.iste.co.uk/pinet/geographic2.zip

In these maps, the representation of uncertainty in the delineation of avalanche zones is based on a qualitative criterion (in this case the delineation method used) as well as on the level of certainty in the delineation of the avalanche zone. This method of representing the spatial uncertainty of the hazard zones complements the previously studied risk intensity representation in the risk prevention plans.

4.5.2. Contributions to the spatial representation of uncertainty

Beyond the use of Jacques Bertin's visual variables, several authors have also proposed original methods for representing the uncertainty of spatial objects, which could be used in the field of natural risk management.

Thus, Alan MacEachren has proposed to extend Jacques Bertin's semiotics rules to represent objects whose locations are uncertain [MAC 05]. In particular, he proposes to use saturation, sharpness, or transparency (Figure 4.14). With saturation, MacEachren proposes that features mapped with a high level of certainty use pure hues, while those with less certainty are represented with a proportionally less saturated color [MAC 05]. Other authors, such as [PAN 09], have also proposed using transparency, area blur and point sharpness to represent uncertainty.

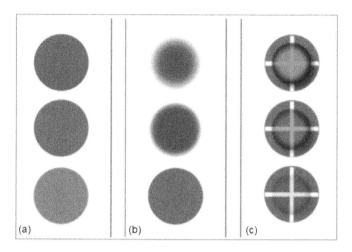

Figure 4.14. *Proposal of uncertainty representation for point data, using intensity (a), blur (b) or transparency (c) [MAC 05]. For a color version of this figure, see www.iste.co.uk/pinet/geographic2.zip*

In the field of natural hazard mapping, methods for representing uncertainty have also been proposed as an extension of Bertin's visual variables [ARN 09].

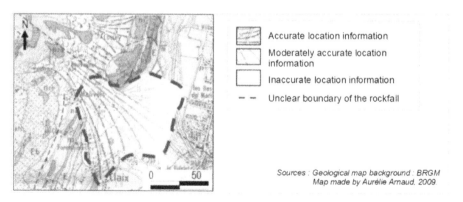

Figure 4.15. *Representation of imprecise boundaries of landslide areas [ARN 09]. For a color version of this figure, see www.iste.co.uk/pinet/geographic2.zip*

In the example of Figure 4.15, transparency and the dotted line (corresponding to the visual variable of the shape) are used to represent imprecise boundaries in the localization of landslides. It has also been proposed in [ARN 09] to extend the graphical semiology to represent uncertainty with cognition rules, especially through the use of pictograms.

More recently, some authors in the field of geovisualization have enriched the methods of representing spatial uncertainty by using original techniques. These include "sketchy" representations, whose use to represent objects with uncertain boundaries can be particularly suitable [W00 12], as illustrated in Figure 4.16.

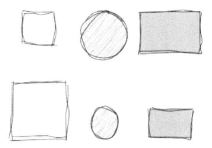

Figure 4.16. *Representation of objects with uncertain contours by using "sketchy" representation styles [WOO 12]*

The methods of uncertainty representation proposed here constitute original contributions to cartography, which must nevertheless be confronted with the perception and understanding that they imply for operational users. These contributions are thus tracks to be experimented in the field of natural hazards representation, and whose impact in terms of perception and decision making must be evaluated.

4.6. Conclusion

Natural hazards are by definition uncertain phenomena, and the delineation of hazard areas in hazard maps is therefore subject to significant spatial uncertainty. The uncertainty associated with this delimitation is mainly caused by three parameters: the intensity of the hazard, the data used to model it and the associated methods. In the hazard maps associated with risk prevention plans, only the intensity of the hazard is taken into account to qualify the uncertainty in the delimitation of the danger zone. The uncertainty associated with the data and modeling methods can be considered to be nonexistent. Only a few maps (such as the Avalanche Occurrence Maps) incorporate a formal representation of uncertainty in the spatial delineation of the hazard through the differentiation of the delineation methods used and the level of certainty in the delineation. None of the maps analyzed actually indicate the uncertainty associated with the geographic data used.

In terms of cartographic representation, the analysis of hazard maps in PPRNs shows that the use of the visual variable of color remains in the majority. This is to the detriment of visual variables, such as the value, which are considered more suitable for representing the uncertainty associated with the intensity of the hazard. Thus, the representation methods proposed in these hazard maps are mainly inspired by the theory of the egg yolk [COH 96] when the number of hazard classes is low, or by a discrete representation of fuzzy objects when the number of hazard classes is higher.

In general, the heterogeneity of the representations of hazard intensity and the underlying danger zones suggests that a broader reflection should be carried out in order to standardize the criteria for uncertainty representation in the delimitation of danger zones, as well as the associated graphic representation rules. Such a harmonization would benefit both crisis managers and the general public by building a common cartographic culture.

Moreover, the innovative methods of uncertainty representation proposed in recent years in the field of geovisualization have not yet been mobilized in an operational context to represent natural hazards, which are uncertain phenomena by definition. A reflection on the value of these methods of representing uncertainty in the field of risk management must continue to be carried out in order to evaluate their potential benefits in terms of crisis preparation and management.

4.7. References

[ARN 09] ARNAUD A., Valorisation de l'information dédiée aux évènements de territoires à risque. Une application cartographique et géovisualisation de la couronne grenobloise, PhD Thesis, Université Joseph Fourier, Saint-Martin-d'Hères, 2009.

[BAR 14] BARSALOU M.A., *Root Cause Analysis: A Step-By-Step Guide to Using the Right Tool at the Right Time*, CRC Press, New York, 2014.

[BAT 19] BATTON-HUBERT M., PINET F., "Formalisms and representations of imperfect geographic objects", in BATTON-HUBERT M., DESJARDIN E., PINET F. (eds), *Geographic Data Imperfection 1: From Theory to Applications*, ISTE Ltd, London, and John Wiley & Sons, New York, 2019.

[BOR 94] BORREL G., "La carte de localisation probable des avalanches", *M@ppemonde*, pp.17–19, 1994.

[BER 67] BERTIN J., *Sémiologie graphique. Les diagrammes, les réseaux, les cartes*, Gauthier-Villars, Paris, 1967.

[CHE 04] CHESNEAU E., "Propositions pour une cartographie du risque", *Bulletin du Comité français de cartographie*, vol. 181, pp. 50–70, 2004.

[COH 96] COHN A.G., GOTTS N.M., "The 'egg-yolk' representation of regions with intermediate boundaries", in BURROUGH P., FRANCK A.U. (eds), *Geographic Objects with Intermediate Boundaries*, Taylor and Francis, London, 1996.

[FED 03] FEDERAL OFFICE FOR CIVIL PROTECTION, Swiss integrated risk management cycle, Report, FOCP, 2003.

[FIS 91] FISHER P.F., "Modeling and visualizing uncertainty in geographic data", in BEARD K., BUTTENFIELD B.P., CLAPHAM S.B., *Visualization of Spatial Data Quality*, NCGIA Research Initiative 7, Scientific Report for the Specialist Meeting, Castine, 1991.

[FOL 19] FOLLIN J.-M., GIRRES, J-F., OLTEANU-RAIMOND A.-M. et al., "The origins of imperfection in geographic data", in BATTON-HUBERT M., DESJARDIN E., PINET F. (eds), *Geographic Data Imperfection 1: From Theory to Applications*, ISTE Ltd, London, and John Wiley & Sons, New York, 2019.

[GIR 17] GIRRES J.-F., SOLA G., "Modeling and representation of spatial uncertainty in risk maps. Application to danger areas related to marine submersion hazard", *Proceedings of the 28th International Cartographic Conference (ICC'17)*, July 2–7, Washington, DC, 2017.

[HOP 06] HOPE S., HUNTER G.H., "Testing the effects of positional uncertainty on spatial decision-making", *International Journal of Geographical Information Science*, vol. 21, pp. 21, 2006.

[INR 05] INRAE, Cartes de localisation des phénomènes d'avalanches, available at: https://www.avalanches.fr/static/1public/epaclpa/documents/guides/CLPA_presentation/CLPA_presentation_lire_carte.ppt, 2005.

[JON 01] JONES R., CAWOOD M., DURHAM K., "An Australian innovation in emergency risk management", *International Journal of Risk Assessment and Management*, vol. 2, nos 3/4, pp. 288–302, 2001.

[LEO 10] LEONE F., MESCHINET DE RICHEMOND N., VINET F., *Aléas naturels et gestion des risques*, Presses Universitaires de France, Paris, 2010.

[MAC 05] MACEACHREN A., ROBINSON A., HOPPER S. et al., "Visualizing geospatial information uncertainty: What we know and what we need to know", *Cartography and Geographic Information Science*, vol. 32, no. 3, pp. 139–160, 2005.

[PAN 08] PANG A., "Visualizing uncertainty in natural hazards", in BOSTROM A., FRENCH S., GOTTIEB S. (eds), *Risk Assessment, Modeling and Decision Support*, Springer, Berlin, Heidelberg, 2008.

[PIN 10] PINET F., Modélisation des contraintes d'intégrité dans les systèmes d'information environnementaux, Habilitation à Diriger les Recherches, Université Blaise Pascal, Paris, 2010.

[PRE 12] PREFECTURE DU GARD, Plan de Prévention des Risques Inondation – La cartographie de l'aléa de référence, available at: http://www.gard.gouv.fr/Politiques-publiques/Securite-et-protection-de-la-population/Risques/Gestion-du-risque-inondation/Plans-de-Prevention-du-Risque-Inondation-PPRI/Les-PPRI-approuves, 2012.

[PRE 14] PREFECTURE DE LOIRE-ATLANTIQUE, Cartographie des aléas littoraux en Loire-Atlantique dans le cadre des futurs PPRL, available at: https://www.loire-atlantique.gouv.fr/content/download/15876/101238/file/V7_ref20_aleas_secteur_guerande_st_nazaire_JUR_pages1_15.pdf, 2014.

[SOL 16] SOLA G., Représentation cartographique de l'incertitude appliquée aux risques naturels, Geomatics Master's Thesis, AgroParisTech, Paris, 2016.

[TAC 09] TACNET J.-M., Prise en compte de l'incertitude dans l'expertise des risques naturels en montagne par analyse multicritères et fusion d'information, PhD Thesis in Environmental Sciences, École Nationale Supérieure des Mines de Saint-Étienne, Saint-Étienne, 2009.

[UNI 04] UNITED NATIONS DEVELOPMENT PROGRAM, Reducing disaster risk. A challenge for development, Report, UNDP – Bureau for Crisis Prevention and Recovery, New York, 2004.

[WOO 12] WOOD J., ISENBERG P., ISENBERG T. et al., "Sketchy rendering for information visualization", *IEEE Transactions on Visualization and Computer Graphics*, vol. 18, no. 12, pp. 2749–2758, 2012.

[ZAD 76] ZADEH L.A., "A fuzzy-algorithmic approach to the definition of complex or imprecise concepts", in BOSSEL H., KLACZKO S., MÜLLER N. (eds), *Systems Theory in the Social Sciences*, Springer-Birkhäuser, Basel, 1976.

Incorporating Uncertainty Into Victim Location Processes in the Mountains: A Methodological, Software and Cognitive Approach

5.1. Introduction

When someone (the victim themselves or a third party) calls for help for an injured or lost person in the mountains, one of the tasks that rescue workers have to perform during this call is to identify where the victim is located, with sufficient accuracy in the order of a few tens of meters. This type of referencing is commonly used by people in everyday life. Chapter 7 of this book shows another use of this type of referencing in the description of itineraries for visually impaired people. The work of the ANR CHOUCAS[1] project has allowed us, among other things, to propose a spatial reasoning model [BUN 19, BUN 21a] and a geovisualization environment dedicated to the search for victims in mountains [VIR 19, VIR 21], integrated through two interconnected prototypes called RUITOR and GASPAR, respectively. This chapter describes how the uncertainty and imperfection inherent to the process of locating a victim in the mountains have been taken into account in these two elements of the project.

Chapter written by Matthieu VIRY, Mattia BUNEL, Marlène VILLANOVA, Ana-Maria OLTEANU-RAIMOND, Cécile DUCHÊNE and Paule-Annick DAVOINE.

1 ANR CHOUCAS: Integration of heterogeneous data and spatial reasoning for victim location assistance in the mountains. ANR-16-CE23-0018, Viry M., Bunel M., Villanova M., Olteanu-Raimond A.-M., Duchêne C., Davoine P.-A.

Four main scientific issues are addressed in this work. The first one concerns the translation of a cue verbally expressed by the caller, such as "I am on a ridge", into a localization element expressed in an indirect frame of reference, in which we clearly identified a subject to be localized (here the victim – "I"), a spatial relation (here "on") and a landmark object or a type of landmark object (here the "ridge" type). The second problem concerns the translation of a location element expressed in an indirect reference frame into a zone known as a *compatible location zone* (CLZ), expressed in a direct spatial reference frame (given reference coordinate system), and then the merging of several CLZs (corresponding to several cues) into a *probable location zone* (PLZ), which is the zone in which the victim is supposed to be located in terms of a set of cues. The third problem concerns the taking the imperfection and uncertainty that weigh on the different clues given by the person who calls for help into account. Finally, the fourth problem concerns the visual restitution of a zone of compatible or probable detection by translating the associated imperfection and uncertainty.

As it is ultimately about developing a prototype to support the reasoning made by the rescuer, the treatment of these problems is based on the following components: (1) the development of an interface (section 5.3) facilitating the acquisition of cues, by collecting the associated uncertainty, and allowing their translation in the form of expected parameters by so-called spatialization methods; (2) a set of spatialization methods allowing (i) an indirect referencing to be translated into a CLZ modeled by a vague region expressed in a direct referential and (ii) several CLZs to merge into a PLZ (section 5.4); (3) appropriate visualization choices for the representation of vague regions, as computed by the previous methods and aiming to favor informed reasoning by the rescuer (section 5.5); (4) thus, uncertainty management is shared between the rescuer and the software components (interface and processing).

Sections 5.3–5.5 detail the methodological aspects and the implementation of each component of the approach based on an example serving as a red thread and corresponding to a real alert case, called "Grand Veymont Alert", described in Box 5.1 and Figure 5.1. Section 5.2 presents the sources of the imperfection that must be taken into account in the application case of victim location in the mountains. Section 5.6 summarizes the results obtained and opens up perspectives for the future.

The person who contacts the emergency services, known as the caller, is in this case a mountain leader. He is next to the victim, who is one of his clients. The caller begins by indicating that he has climbed the Grand Veymont (Vercors Massif, Alps, France) with his clients and that they are in the process of descending. We describe here a passage of dialogue between the rescuer and the caller that contains four clues stated verbally by the caller:

"Rescuer: Are you between Grand Veymont and Pas de la Ville?

Caller: I am between the Grand Veymont (...) and Pas de la Ville, right on the south side.

Rescuer: On the south side of Pas de la Ville?

Caller: No, sorry, north side.

Rescuer: Are you beyond Pas de la Ville? Between Pas de la Ville and Pierre Blanche?

Caller: Yes, I am beyond the Pas de la Ville (...) On a small meadow.

Rescuer: How far are you from Pas de la Ville?

Caller: About a half mile, I think, as the crow flies".

Figure 5.1 shows a map of the situation, including the summits of Grand Veymont, Pierre Blanche and Pas de la Ville.

It can be noted that the first two indications are contradictory: according to the situation map, it is clear that the victim cannot be between Grand Veymont and Pas de la Ville and between Pas de la Ville and Pierre Blanche at the same time. Presumably, it is the second situation that is true. But as the caller was also very affirmative in his first indication (even if he went back on it later), and as it is not rare according to the rescue workers and the corpus of alerts that we dispose of to see someone change their mind several times, we keep the two possibilities, with a stronger level of doubt on the first one. Furthermore, we do not have a geographic reference of grasslands in our data. We therefore partially exploit the indication "I am on a small meadow" by considering that the victim is not in a forest. From this dialogue excerpt, we therefore retain four clues (which call upon three location relations), which we reformulate as follows:

1) the victim is between Grand Veymont and Pas de la Ville (indication considered very uncertain);

2) the victim is between Pas de la Ville and Pierre Blanche;

3) the victim is not in a forest;

4) the victim is 800 m from Pas de la Ville (indication considered not completely certain).

Box 5.1. *"Grand Veymont" alert*

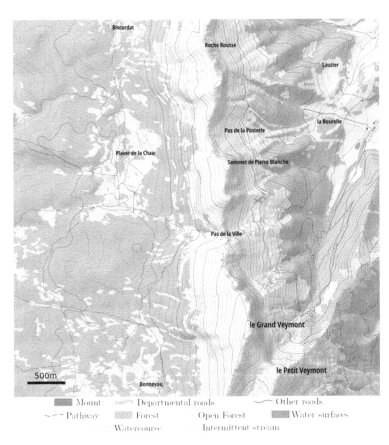

Figure 5.1. *Situation map for the Grand Veymont Alert. For a color version of this figure, see www.iste.co.uk/pinet/geographic2.zip*

5.2. Sources of imperfection

Follin et al. [FOL 19] identify five sources of imperfection in the process of acquisition, analysis and visualization of geographic information: the initial source, the target model, the measurement instrument, the operating mode and the operator. In the case of victim location in the mountains, the five sources of imperfection appear in a direct or indirect way in the decision-making process. Next, we review the sources of imperfection encountered in the case of mountain rescue. In this analysis, we identify three types of imperfection more precisely, namely imprecision, uncertainty, and incompleteness, a classification well known in the literature [BOU 95, OLT 09, DEV 19]. The imprecision qualifies knowledge or data. In a general way, it concerns the difficulty of expressing a state of reality by an expressed knowledge clearly and precisely ("the victim is big", "I am at about 1 km from the parking lot"). When imprecision concerns geographical data, it is called spatial imprecision and expresses the difficulty of defining (i.e. assigning a semantic to it) or delimiting the limits of a geographical object [BUN 21b]. Uncertainty refers to the doubt that we have about the truthfulness of knowledge. Finally, incompleteness refers to the lack of knowledge or partial knowledge or lack of data.

In this section, we describe the types of imperfections characterizing the initial sources. The other sources of imperfections mentioned in [FOL 19] will be presented in the other sections.

5.2.1. *Imprecision in location expression associated with a clue*

A location clue is expressed by an applicant using natural language such as "I am under a power line", "the victim has been walking for three hours from the parking lot" and "I see the Lac Blanc". Bunel et al. [BUN 19] formalize the location clue through three elements: the subject ("I", "the victim"), the reference object which can be named ("Lac Blanc") or unnamed ("parking lot", "power line") and the locational relation ("under", "walking from", "seeing").

Imprecision can be identified at the level of the locational relation (e.g. close to), since the notion of "close" can be interpreted differently from one victim to another. It can also be identified at the level of reference objects as real-world entities, but also at the level of the geometric representation and semantic description of reference objects materialized in a geographic database (e.g. the limits of a forest are imprecise, the representation of a valley through a point is imprecise). In addition, we have identified elements of language that may be imprecise. For example, in the location clues "I see a large elongated lake", "I am about 500 m from the Barre des Écrins", the expressions "large", "elongated" and "about" are sources of imprecision. The consideration of imprecision in the formalizing of localization and in the method of spatialization seems essential to us, to both avoid ignoring areas where the victim could be (false positives) and avoid overestimating the localization area (false negatives), which could lead to a wrong assumption by the rescuer. As discussed in [BUN 21b], in addition to being imprecise, locational relations can result in varying degrees of imprecision, although the meaning is close. Thus, for example, for the two location clues "I am close to Grenoble" and "I am in the vicinity of Grenoble" the semantics are similar, since both clues express the proximity of the victim to the object of reference, in this case, the city of Grenoble. Without evaluating the degree of imprecision in detail, we can say that in the case of these two relations, the locational relation "in the vicinity of" is generally perceived as more imprecise than the relation "near". The analysis of the semantics of the locational relations and the estimation of their imprecision thus seem to be of primary importance for the definition of spatialization methods.

5.2.2. *Uncertainty in location expression associated with a clue*

Location clues can also be marked by uncertainty, which leads us to say that they can be false or partially false. Indeed, several causes are at the origin of this uncertainty, for example, the lack of knowledge of the terrain by the victim, the state of health of the victim, fear and stress, or lack of expertise on the mountain. Sometimes, the victim clearly expresses their uncertainty through expressions that convey doubt: "I think" and "in my opinion". In most cases, the location clue may be false without the victim realizing it. This situation is more difficult to identify and take into account for the spatialization of location clues.

Given the complexity of identifying uncertainty, our approach is to rely on the rescuer, their expertise and knowledge of the terrain to judge the veracity of a location clue. Depending on the victim's condition and knowledge of the terrain, the rescuer will be able to identify the relevance and veracity of a clue more easily. Thus, when the rescuer has doubts about the veracity of a clue, they can ask additional questions in order to decide whether the clue expressed can be taken into account in the location process. The veracity of the initial clue can be questioned at any time by a new clue given by the victim or the merging of clues. The rescuer can therefore change the degree of uncertainty later if necessary.

5.2.3. *Incompleteness of geographical data*

We mentioned above that the victim locates themself via landmark objects. Concerning the incompleteness, it is obvious that the description based on clues provided by the applicant cannot be exhaustive (it is indeed illusory to imagine that the victim is located in relation to all the possible reference objects). We are therefore working with an incomplete description of the situation, and each new clue, if it is true and relevant, contributes to making it a little less incomplete. Incompleteness should also be considered from the point of view of the data sources used in the processing of the alert. The landmark objects are materialized through geographic objects in institutional (e.g. BDTOPO) or collaborative (e.g. CamptoCamp and OpenStreetMap) databases. Despite the proposed multi-source geographic data integration [GEN 21], the victim may indicate the location relative to a landmark object that, although visible on the ground, does not exist in the integrated database. If the geographical object is named, for example "I am near the Ruissant waterfall", the rescuer may realize that this landmark object (here Ruissant waterfall) is missing in the integrated database. On the other hand, when the landmark object indicated by the victim is not named (e.g. "I am under a power line"), the rescuer has no prior information on the fact that all geographical objects such as power lines are well represented in the integrated database, in the same way that they do not know if geographical objects exist in the database used, but that certain power lines no longer exist in the field.

Both of these cases are problematic and can generate false positives or false negatives, wrongly reducing the localization area, or on the contrary, wrongly increasing it. The management of incompleteness will be done both at the interface level (section 5.3) and at the localization process level (section 5.4).

5.3. Detecting uncertainty and imprecision in the interface

As mentioned in the introduction, one of the objectives of the CHOUCAS project is to develop a prototype that aims to support the reasoning operated by the rescuer when locating a victim. More precisely, it is about proposing an interface facilitating the transcription and treatment of the localization clues, subject to imperfections, collected during the dialogue with the requester. Before addressing the interface components dedicated to this (section 5.3.2), we introduce the underlying data models. They take the form of ontologies developed within the CHOUCAS project, including concepts allowing the formalization of an alert. Detailed descriptions of these ontologies are proposed in [OLT 20, VIR 20]. We focus here on the way the concepts allow the management of the imperfections mentioned in the previous section.

5.3.1. *Formalization of an alert according to the ontologies of the CHOUCAS project*

Our study of the context and analysis of the needs carried out within the framework of the project led us to propose a system of three ontologies:

1) The Ontology of Landmark Objects (OOR) [OLT 20] organizes the concepts describing a territory into a total of 458 classes, which specialize in the following five main classes: "Construction" covers human constructions whose apparent function does not allow them to be attached to the hydrography, vegetation and relief classes; "Hydrography" covers hydrographic elements and constructions whose apparent function is related to hydrography; "Terrain" covers the particular elements of terrain: "Vegetation" covers vegetation, whether natural or artificial; "Zoning" covers the immaterial delimitations of the territory, which may be de facto (agglomeration) or de jure (municipality, industrial zone).

2) The Ontology of Locational Relations (ORL) [BUN 21a] identifies 51 locational relations used in the context of describing a position in the mountains. In particular, the relations allow the position of the victim to be expressed with respect to a concept derived from the ORL. Some of the relations proposed in the OOR intrinsically carry the imprecision with which the requester expresses themselves (like orl#Around, orl#near).

3) The Ontology of Choucas Alert (OAC) [VIR 20] is an application ontology dedicated to the formalization of the alert phase of victim localization in the mountains operated by rescue workers. This ontology formalizes the concepts involved in the processing of an alert by a rescuer: it is on these constructs that their reasoning is carried out, operated "in a geovisualization environment".

An *alert*[2] corresponds to the whole process of searching for a victim, from the moment it is triggered by a call from a *requester* (who may or may not be the victim themselves) to its end (corresponding to the discovery of the victim or to the abandonment of the search). A *clue* corresponds to a fragment of speech of the caller, given during their dialogue with the emergency services, describing the position (current or past) of the victim to be located. This concept is central in our model since this fragment of speech is a location clue containing spatial and temporal information. Several of the notions that we introduce hereafter take the uncertainty linked to the notion of a *clue* into account. The OAC also models the credit given to each clue, formalized here under the term *certainty*. The *certainty* granted by the rescuer to a *clue* is a notion that translates the uncertainty on the information provided by the requester. In the end, it is a decision made by the rescuer that results from their impression at the time of the exchanges concerning the information given by the requester (hesitations, disclaimers, etc.), from their knowledge of the field and expertise more generally. One of the ways for the rescuer to reduce this uncertainty is to question the applicant further. If this is not enough to remove doubt, then the *confiance* given to the clue is not total (another option could be to not consider this clue at all).

The other essential element in the formalization of the uncertain information given by the requester is the *locational relation* (from ORL), which links spatial entities (e.g. the victim and a concept from OOR) and is transformable into a corresponding *locational area* (see below). More precisely, a *locational relation* links *spatial entities* through two properties, a *target* and a *site* (where the target is the spatial entity to be located and the site is the spatial entity used as a landmark: the requester describes the position of the target, the victim, with respect to the site). The specificity of the *spatial entities* that we formalize is that they can describe both a specific object from OOR (we speak then of a *landmark spatial entity*, for example the lake of Chambon) and a set of objects (we speak then of *candidate spatial entities*, for example, "the lakes" that we also find in the OOR). This responds to the need to take into account the imprecision encountered when expressing an index (cf. section 5.2.1), depending on whether the applicant explicitly designates an entity (e.g. "the lake of Chambon") or whether they are unable to provide this level of precision (e.g. "a lake"). Thus, speaking of a lake will be understood in our case as "an indeterminate lake among all the existing lakes". This can also respond to the situations mentioned in

2 Concepts in italics are from the Ontology of Choucas Alert.

section 5.2.3 when a named object is absent from the database: we then search for candidate objects, that is, those that are the same type as the named object. The site associated with the spatial relationship will then be a set of candidate spatial entities, "all lakes", so as to necessarily include "the lake" to which the victim refers. Processing an index yields, via a spatialization process (see section 5.4), a CLZ.

Taking the different *clues* given by the requestor in the context of the alert into account is not systematic, but is part of a research *hypothesis*. A *hypothesis* thus corresponds to the consideration of one or more clues: the criteria for retaining or not retaining clues can, for example, be based on the *certainty* that the rescuer places in them. A PLZ is determined by merging CLZs from the considered clues, and thus from the associated CLZs.

In this model, a search hypothesis is necessarily linked to an *initial search area* (ISA): this is a large portion of the territory, defined for each search hypothesis, and in which the search is carried out. It is sufficiently large to be able to consider with certainty that the victim is located there and can be the subject of several location hypotheses. Defining an ISA also makes it possible to restrict the subsequent calculations to this zone only, as its area serves as a boundary box for the spatialization and fusion calculations (section 5.4). For the example described in Box 5.1, the ISA corresponds to the area covered by Figure 5.1.

5.3.2. *Specific acquisition components*

We propose a user interface, GASPAR, dedicated to the processing of an alert and allowing most of the concepts of the project's three ontologies to be materialized. In the workflow that we propose, when an alert is triggered, the rescuer is invited to visually define, in an interactive way, the concerned ISA. Once the ISA is defined, the rescuer can enter the clues collected during the dialogue with the requester.

5.3.2.1. *Creating a clue panel*

The key concepts to be included to characterize a clue are as follows: locational relation, site, certainty, time and duration of validity of the clue. Each of these concepts is collected via a dedicated component, the whole constituting the input panel of a clue, as shown in Figure 5.2. Thus, in the Grand Veymont Alert, when the requester indicates that he is located "between the Grand Veymont and the Pas de la Ville" while expressing doubt about this location element, it is possible for the rescuer to use the certainty cursor to indicate a "low" level of certainty in the clue (Figure 5.2, left). We also note that the locational relation is selected by the user from a list of several dozen. This selection is facilitated by the auto-completion of the relation name (when possible) and by the possibility to filter the spatial relations by type (proximity, contact, orientation, etc.). These types correspond to the abstract classes of the ORL ontology. The other elements of this component also represent concepts defined in the OAC ontology: concepts of *site* of the locational relation (here two sites are necessary because of the nature of the ternary locational relation), of the *instant or duration* at which the clue is valid (here it is simply the temporal information "now"). The two other elements that appear are specific to the user interface that we propose, notably the recall of the clue in natural language corresponding to the fact that the interface proposes to record each clue in a note block type component – not presented here but in [VIR 20] – and the display color of the clue.

The dialogue between the requester and the rescuer leads to the immediate entry of a second clue corresponding to "between Pas de la Ville and Pierre Blanche". This is done in the same way as the previous clue, but by now selecting a "strong" level of certainty. Indeed, the exchanges between the requester and the rescuer have allowed the rescuer to judge that this clue is totally reliable.

A third clue of the alert leads us to capture the information related to the fact that the requester says he is in a grassland. As mentioned in the introduction, we have to manage a case of incomplete data (absence of data delimiting grasslands). The management of this situation is done by negation of the relation "I am in a forest" and thus by using the negation of the function "In planimetric" applied to all forests. Finally, the last clue "at 800 m as the crow flies from Pas de la Ville" is entered into the interface with a "medium" level of certainty (Figure 5.2, right). This level of certainty corresponds to the doubt expressed by the requester about the accuracy of the distance communicated to the rescuer. Selecting the location relationship "quantitative planimetric distance" then brings up an additional input element to specify the distance. This refers to the notion of the *modifier* of the locational relation to be used (a concept of the ORL ontology). The clue creation component thus makes it possible to translate the lack of certainty regarding the clues of an alert, and this at two levels via the input of the level of certainty given to each clue and the selection of a category of objects (e.g. "forests") when the requester is not able to precisely name an object or when it is not possible to name a particular instance.

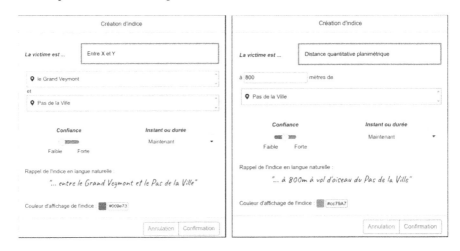

Figure 5.2. *Clue creation panel – first clue (left). Clue creation panel – third clue (right). The system asks where the victim is, the location can be provided and the user can confirm whether they have strong confidence in this information. For a color version of this figure, see www.iste.co.uk/pinet/geographic2.zip*

As the clues are entered and validated, the information specific to each clue is serialized and sent to the spatialization service presented in section 5.4, allowing the corresponding CLZ to be displayed. This information is also reported in the index and hypothesis table.

5.3.2.2. *Table of clues and hypotheses*

The creation of each clue is reflected in a component that we call the table of clues and hypotheses (Figure 5.3), where each line represents a created clue and the information that is specific to it: locational relation, site, level of certainty, hypothesis (selection of the hypothesis via *checkboxes*) and its display mode (element explained in section 5.5).

This component allows the exploration of several hypotheses that indicate the absence of absolute certainty on the alert clues. It allows us to show the contribution of each clue to a search hypothesis and record it. In our example, this component allows the rescuer, as soon as the second clue is given by the requester, to issue a new search hypothesis (the second one in our case), omitting the first clue, but taking the three other clues into account (see the boxes checked in the hypothesis column in Figure 5.3).

	Locational relation	Location	Certainty	Hypothesis 1 2 3	Display
	Between X and Y	le Grand Veymont Pas de la Ville	Low	☑ ☐ ☐	■ ☒
	Between X and Y	Pas de la Ville Pierre Blanche	High	☐ ☑ ☐	■ ☒
	(NOT) In the planimetric plane	Forest (all)	High	☐ ☑ ☐	■ ☒
	Quantitative planimetric distance (800m)	Pas de la Ville	Medium	☐ ☑ ☐	■ ☒

Figure 5.3. *Table of clues and hypotheses. For a color version of this figure, see www.iste.co.uk/pinet/geographic2.zip*

The user interface we propose reacts automatically to the creation of clues and the modifications made to the hypotheses. Indeed, each hypothesis has its own cartographic visualization, allowing the rescuer to compare the hypotheses and display them simultaneously. Moreover, as soon as a hypothesis is composed of two or more clues, they are merged to obtain the victim's PLZ. This PLZ is also displayed in the map dedicated to the corresponding hypothesis.

5.4. Taking imperfection in spatialization into account

In this section, we describe the process of spatialization of a hypothesis (i.e. the construction, from the clues that compose it, of the CLZ associated with each clue and then of the PLZ associated with the hypothesis) and the consideration of the imperfection linked to this process.

5.4.1. *Relationship between CLZ and PLZ and the construction of the PLZ*

As previously mentioned, the PLZ delineates the section(s) of the ISA that corresponds to the different clues retained for the hypothesis under consideration. In other words, any point in the PLZ is correctly described by the set of location clues included in the hypothesis, unlike all other points in the ISA. In a similar way, the CLZs are areas bounding the section(s) of the ISA correctly described by a given location index. It can be noted that there is a strong relationship between CLZ and PLZ. Indeed, each CLZ delimits the area that corresponds to a given clue, while the PLZ delimits the area that corresponds to all clues. The latter is therefore expressible as a composition of the CLZs of the same hypothesis, since it is the zone delimiting the positions belonging to all the CLZs. It is thus constructed as the intersection of the CLZs. We will see later (sections 5.4.3 and 5.4.4) that the CLZs are modeled as fuzzy sets, so their intersection to construct the PLZ is based on the t-norm of fuzzy sets [ZAD 65, BAT 19].

5.4.2. The process of creating CLZs

At this point, according to the proposed method for inputting the requester's information: (1) a hypothesis is composed of a set of clues and (2) when a location clue refers to a set of potential objects and not to a single clearly identified landmark object, for the purpose of calculating its CLZ, it is considered to be composed of several clues, each referring to a single potential object.

The approach used to locate the victim according to a given hypothesis is thus based on a successive decomposition of the information elements into simpler ones. The proposed method to spatialize a location clue, that is, to build its associated CLZ, goes even further in this decomposition approach by adding an additional decomposition step (transparent for the GASPAR user) once a given locational relation and a reference object (landmark or candidate) are identified. This additional step consists, when possible, of decomposing the locational relation considered into a set of so-called atomic locational relations. The notion of an atomic locational relation is based on the idea that two different locational relations can have common characteristic elements that constitute composable semantic bricks [BUN 19]. Thus, in the Grand Veymont Alert, the locational relations "Planimetric quantitative distance" and "In planimetric" used for clues (3) and (4) are not decomposable, but the relation "Between x and y" used for clues (1) and (2) is: it is considered to be equivalent to the conjunction of two instances of an atomic relation called "In the direction of x from y", in which x and y are reversed. In other words, being between x and y is considered equivalent to being in the direction of x from y and in the direction of y from x. The atomic relation "In the direction of x from y", which can also be used on its own, generalizes the notion of a cardinal relation with a direction that is not one of the cardinal directions, but the half-line joining x to y.

Once a location clue has been decomposed, if necessary, into several sub-clues associated with the different candidate objects and then according to the atomic locational relations, two main steps are necessary to construct the associated CLZ [BUN 19]: (1) it calculates the elementary CLZ associated with each sub-clue, that is, each pair (atomic locational relation, candidate object) (this calculation method is the subject of section 5.4.3); (2) it recomposes the CLZ from these elementary CLZs by intersection of the elementary CLZs associated with the different atomic relations of the same candidate object, and then by union of the CLZs obtained in this way for all the candidate objects. Using a union for the CLZs associated with the different candidate objects is justified by the fact that the locational relation must be verified with one OR the other of the candidate objects. The union is done using the t-conorm [ZAD 65, BAT 19].

5.4.3. *Taking imprecision into account*

The solution chosen to take the inherent imprecision of the clues into account (see section 5.2) was to use the fuzzy logic formalism [ZAD 65] to define the CLZ and PLZ in a non-bivalent way. The fuzzy logic formalism allows each position in a space to be assigned a so-called degree of membership (between 0 and 1), quantifying the veracity of the locational clue. The positions with a zero degree of membership are those that do not correspond to the clue (and are therefore outside the locational zone), those with a degree of membership of 1 correspond to the clue (and are therefore in the locational zone), and the positions that have a degree of membership between 0 and 1 (excluded) partially validate the locational clue and therefore partially belong to the locational zone thus defined. For theoretical aspects, we refer the reader to Volume 1 [BAT 19]. In terms of implementation, the CLZ and PLZ are modeled as fuzzy rasters covering the ISA. This is similar to what Bloch [BLO 96] calls "Fuzzy Landscape".

The construction of the CLZ spatializing a locational clue referring to a given reference object (candidate or landmark) is performed using a three-step method: rasterization of the reference object, computation of a dedicated metric and fuzzification [BUN 21a, p. 163].

During the rasterization step, the reference object is rasterized. Depending on the locational relation considered, the entire geometry of the object is rasterized, or only a part of it (border, centroid).

The second step of the CLZ construction process is the computation of a dedicated metric for each pixel of the ISA. The chosen metric is a quantity that reflects the semantics of the considered locational relation. For example, for the locational relation "Planimetric quantitative distance", which appears in the Grand Veymont Alert, the metric used is the Euclidean distance of the pixel considered to the rasterized reference object. For the atomic locational relation "In the direction of x from y", resulting from the decomposition of the relation "Between x and y", the metric is the angular deviation between the half-line joining y to x and the half-line joining y to the pixel considered.

The third step of the spatialization process is the so-called fuzzification phase. It is during this third step that the CLZ spatializing the processed clue is really built. The role of this step is to transform the values of the metric into a degree of membership quantifying the membership of a pixel to the CLZ. By defining how a metric value is transformed into a degree of membership, it allows us to give a different meaning to two identical metrics. For example, consider the case where a Euclidean distance metric is computed from the same site. If we use a fuzzyficator that assigns a high degree of membership to small distances and a low degree of membership to large distances, this allows us to spatialize locational clues such as "I am close to...". Conversely, if we apply a fuzzyficator to the previous metric, assigning low membership degrees to small distances and a high membership degree to large distances, then we are able to spatialize locational clues such as "I am far from...". For the relation "Quantitative planimetric distance" which appears in the Grand Veymont Alert, the fuzzifier assigns a maximum degree of membership to pixels for which the calculated Euclidean distance is equal to the distance value entered in the GASPAR interface (800 m here), and this degree decreases linearly on both sides of this value with a slope to be specified (parameter, fixed at 250 m in our case). A fuzzifier of the same form is used for the relationship "In the direction of x from y": the degree of membership is maximal when the computed angular deviation is zero, and decreases linearly to zero at $\pm\alpha$, a parameterizable angle fixed at 90° here. This modeling amounts to mixing the angular sector and half-plane approaches presented by Frank [FRA 92] as used to model directional relations. Thus, by choosing a rasterization method, a metric and a suitable fuzzyficator, we are able to spatialize the set of locational relations used in the context of mountain rescue.

5.4.4. *Taking uncertainty and incompleteness into account*

As presented so far, our spatialization method transforms a set of locational clues referring to a landmark object or candidate objects into a fuzzy locational area. However, this approach only allows us to model imprecision. To allow for the uncertainty of the clue, we allowed the user to define a value of certainty, which is taken into account when computing the results. A qualitative value of certainty can be defined in the GASPAR interface (see Figure 5.2). The rescuer can modify the level of certainty for each clue, but they cannot define the level of certainty according to the position treated, the same level of certainty applies for the whole clue. To deal with this value of certainty, we used possibility theory [ZAD 78, BAT 19], which extends fuzzy logic to allow for joint modeling of uncertainty and imprecision. When applied to the process previously described, this theory allows us to ensure that clues defined as uncertain by the rescuer will not lead to positions being removed from the PLZ. Thus, for a position to be considered as not belonging to the PLZ, it is necessary that a locational clue is qualified as "certain" and sets its degree of membership to zero.

As for incompleteness, it is not taken into account by means of a specific theory, or by a modification of the approach previously presented. However, we have made certain modeling choices, which, while not proposing a model of incompleteness, allow us to limit its effects. First, we have chosen to adopt an approach based on open world reasoning. Therefore, we consider that the only information we can process to build the PLZ is the information explicitly given by the requester. It would have been possible to consider all information that is not given by the requester to be false. This approach, closed-world reasoning, has the advantage of being able to infer a large amount of information, but it quickly runs into the problem of incompleteness: each piece of information left out leads to inferring a wrong locational clue. The choice of an open world approach has the double advantage of avoiding this problem, but also of indirectly facilitating the definition of the spatialization method, since it is not necessary to add an inference process. The second mechanism for limiting the effects of incompleteness is the choice that was made to leave a large place for the rescuers in the spatialization process, as discussed in section 5.3. The rescuer is therefore able to perform an initial verification, optimization and disambiguation task. In the case of the clue, "I am in a meadow", knowing that the integrated database does not contain reference objects of the meadow type but does contain objects of the forest type can thus lead the rescuer to transform the clue into: "I am not in a forest". The rescuer can also ask for clarifications, which can lead to defining new locational clues or to completing them. If we cannot speak of "processing incompleteness", we can nevertheless assume that the rescuer tends to reduce it, which, combined with open-world modeling, allows an exogenous consideration of incompleteness.

5.5. Restoring uncertainty in the interface

Visually restoring geospatial uncertainty or blurring to a user is considered useful [KOR 19]. It can even be considered a matter of certainty in the transmission of information. Moreover, it seems all the more important to address the issue of uncertainty restitution as the decision-making process is influenced by the representation of it [HOP 07, RIV 14]. Therefore, and in order to avoid misinterpretation of the represented data (this is sometimes the case, for example, when the probable path of tornadoes is represented, see [RUG 16]), we have chosen to propose and experiment using several visualization methods for spatialized and merged data resulting from the methods described in section 5.4.

5.5.1. *"Classic" solution*

In particular, the visual representation of CLZs and PLZs is a difficult issue. Indeed, the method proposed by Bunel [BUN 21a] (see section 5.4.) produces continuous locational zones represented as raster data. While this data format has a double methodological and semantic interest, it complicates the graphical representation of the results.

The "classic" mode of representation of the rasters exploits the visual variable called "value" by varying the perceived brightness of the pixel to represent the quantity associated with it. We then obtain a representation in gray levels, or a color gradient. Although very effective, this mode of representation poses some difficulties for the representation of locational zones. Indeed, each pixel is assigned a tint, making it opaque when the level of certainty is total. The representation thus obtained has good coverage, and it is difficult to read the information to which it is added. However, the locational zones produced by the method described above cannot help emergency workers make a decision if the contextual elements given by the background map are not visible. The objective is that the locational zones produced, represented on a topographic background map which represents multiple landmarks, allow us to keep a good visualization of the terrain.

A first solution is to represent the locational zones using the value variable, but with a slight transparency, which allows additional information to be perceived through the first information layer (Figure 5.4).

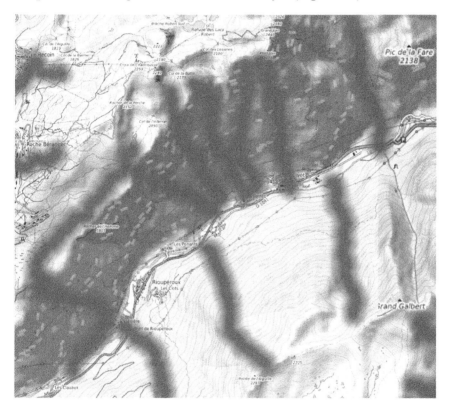

Figure 5.4. *Example of the masking of the map background by the rendering of a CLZ (corresponding to the clue "near a stream") using transparency: map background OpenStreetMap. For a color version of this figure, see www.iste.co.uk/ pinet/geographic2.zip*

This solution is generally quite effective, but it proved unsatisfactory in our case. Indeed, all the colors that we experimented with either tended to mask a significant part of the topographic background or were unreadable. Thus, a variation of blue hides the hydrography (see Figure 5.4), a variation of green blends in with the vegetation, a variation of yellow is unreadable and variations of red and violet, which give the best results, are not very readable. Gray offers the best readability; however, this variation also has a strong negative effect. By superimposing itself on the shading of the topographic background, this variation prevents the intuitive perception of the morphology usually allowed by the shading, which significantly complicates the understanding of the morphology of the terrain. All these solutions are therefore not fully satisfactory, since they significantly mask part of the information necessary for the interpretation of the locational zones.

5.5.2. *Solution based on figures of varying sizes*

The solution adopted by Bunel [BUN 21a] was to represent this same information using the visual variable "size". Here, the data are represented using a figure (generally a circle or a square) whose surface is proportional to the represented value. From a perceptual point of view, we therefore play on the effect of the salience of the largest pixels. However, whereas the representation by variation of value always fills the whole pixel and sees its luminosity vary, the representation by variation of size has an invariant luminosity and a variable extent. Thus, when the represented value decreases, the first mode of representation lets the information superimposed on the pixel appear in a less altered way (the luminosity decreases), whereas the representation using a size variation lets more of the superimposed information appear (the surface of the figure decreases). These two types of representation are illustrated in Figure 5.5.

This second representation mode seems superior to the first one, because what is visible is still accurately represented, contrary to the first solution, where all the information remains visible (except for the very large values) but is altered. The result is a lower visual overlap, and therefore a better readability of the topographic map background.

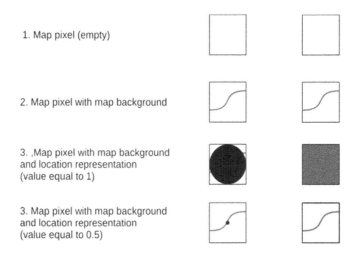

Figure 5.5. *Comparison of solutions based on the use of transparency and symbol size. For a color version of this figure, see www.iste.co.uk/pinet/geographic2.zip*

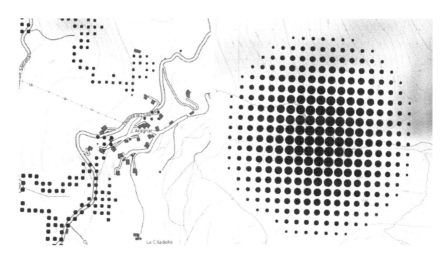

Figure 5.6. *Example of possible confusion between the figures and the elements of the map background: map background OpenTopoMap (left); loss of detailed information of the area of interest by densification of masking (right): OpenTopoMap map background (OpenStreetMap contributors, SRTM). For a color version of this figure, see www.iste.co.uk/pinet/geographic2.zip*

However, in some cases, this representation has various disadvantages. For example, Figure 5.6 (left) shows that it is sometimes possible to confuse the figures with the background map elements (here with the buildings). Figure 5.6 (right) illustrates a difficulty in perceiving the detail of the background map of the area of greatest interest (where the large figures reflect the greatest probability of the victim's presence). Therefore, we propose a combined representation of the information translating the uncertainty, exploiting in particular the capacities of dynamic restitution after a user interaction or those related to a change of zoom level at which the information is consulted.

5.5.3. *Solution by combining representations*

If these methodological considerations make sense when producing static maps, our production context is different since these representations are proposed in a highly interactive geovisualization user interface. Interaction can then be a way to overcome the previous limitations, as shown below. Moreover, these methodological considerations, valid for the representation of a single layer of data, are even more marked when it comes to displaying several layers simultaneously. The nature of the PLZs obtained reinforces this aspect: indeed, the PLZs correspond to the merging of the CLZs of the clues. Thus, the PLZ for a given hypothesis is necessarily superimposed on the representations (i.e. the CLZs) of the clues for this hypothesis, making visual occlusion inevitable.

We thus propose to combine the representations discussed above and modify them according to the context (i.e. according to the information already displayed on the map and the visualization scale).

First, we propose to display each clue using the transparency technique, and this as soon as the result of the calculation of a locational zone is available. In order to facilitate the perception of the boundaries of the clue areas, we also display a line symbolizing the contour of the created area. We believe that the combination of the contour line with the raster makes it easier to perceive the parts of the territory belonging to the CLZ. When we obtain a PLZ, we choose to represent the CLZs only with their respective contours (as illustrated in the following section on the Grand Veymont Alert, see Figure 5.9). Indeed, on the one hand, the PLZ is in essence a zone of superposition (and therefore of occlusion), and on the other hand, the PLZ is the most interesting zone to present to the rescuer since it is the one that is supposed to contain the victim and towards which the intervention must be launched. However, the choice to keep the default display of the CLZ outline makes it possible to perceive the role of each of the CLZs in the resulting PLZ. This can encourage the rescuer to make a new hypothesis that does not take a particular clue into account, because, for example, they consider that it reduces the obtained PLZ too much.

We also propose two display modes for the PLZs, this time depending on the current display resolution. Indeed, we make the assumption that the rescuer is not interested in the same pieces of information, depending on the display scale used in the map component. When the map component is at a low display resolution and contains the whole ISA (see Figure 5.7), we believe that the priority is to show the rescuer where the PLZ is located within the ISA, and this, without any uncertainty restitution effect. The case discussed in the figure corresponds to an "overview" type of information intake by the rescuer and allows the rescuer, for example, to better apprehend situations in which the PLZ is split into several fragments within the ISA.

On the other hand, when the display resolution corresponds to a zoom on the PLZ or one of its fragments, it is useful to be as explicit as possible in what is presented to the rescuer. In this case, we choose to switch to the proportional symbol representation presented earlier (see Figure 5.6, right).

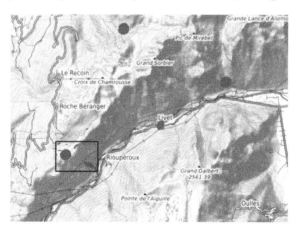

Figure 5.7. *Overview of the ISA and fragments of the PLZ (in red), calculated from three indices: "below the elevation of the Rocher de l'Homme", "near a stream" and "near a waterfall". The black box delimits a zone used later in the text: OpenTopoMap map background (OpenStreetMap contributors, SRTM). For a color version of this figure, see www.iste.co.uk/pinet/geographic2.zip*

Figure 5.8. *Detailed view of three fragments of the PLZ (represented in proportional symbols). Zoom in on the area at the bottom left of Figure 5.7: OpenTopoMap map background (OpenStreetMap contributors, SRTM). For a color version of this figure, see www.iste.co.uk/pinet/geographic2.zip*

5.5.4. *Illustration of the Grand Veymont Alert*

We return to our red line example to illustrate and discuss some of the proposed renderings for processing this alert. Figure 5.9(A) shows the use of the solution combining the display of (i) the contour of the PLZ corresponding to the second clue (being "between Pas de la Ville and Pierre Blanche") and (ii) the transparency effect inside the PLZ, inversely proportional to the probability that the victim is at each point (the more opaque the zone, the higher the probability). The rescuer thus visualizes a zone between the two locations mentioned. We notice that the CLZ generated for the relationship "between x and y" extends quite far on both sides of the axis connecting the two reference points. This is related to the spatialization method chosen for the atomic localization relation "In the direction of x from y", on which the relation "Between x and y" is based (see sections 1.4.2 and 1.4.3), and in particular to the angular deviation value of ±90° chosen as the threshold value to set the degree of membership to the CLZ to 0. It would be possible to reduce this threshold angular distance so as not to generate possible positions too far from the segment joining the two reference objects, but the risk would then be to wrongly exclude some possible positions where the victim could be, if the followed route makes detours around the segment connecting the two reference objects near object

y. We prefer to keep positions far from this segment, but with a low degree of membership, so that they are not excluded from the final PLZ if the other clues do not rule them out, but rather appear in it with a low degree of membership that will lead the rescuer to not favor them. The representations of the other clues are also shown here (Figure 5.9(B) and (C)) and demonstrate the diversity of CLZ shapes resulting from the spatial relationships involved.

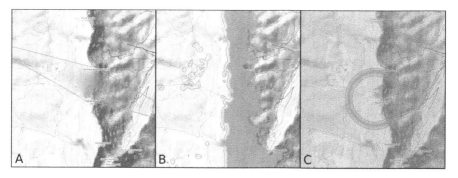

Figure 5.9. *Display (contour + transparency) of the CLZs corresponding to (A) the second clue "between Pas de la ville and Pierre Blanche summit", (B) the third clue "not in the forest" and (C) the fourth clue "at 800 m from Pas de la Ville": OpenTopoMap map background (OpenStreetMap contributors, SRTM). For a color version of this figure, see www.iste.co.uk/pinet/geographic2.zip*

When all the CLZs are taken into account for the calculation of the PLZ, it is shown to the rescuer in several ways:

– Through an overview of the PLZ and its constituent fragments (Figure 5.10).

– When the rescuer zooms in on a part of the PLZ by a representation combining the principle of uncertainty restitution by proportional circles with a color gradient (Figure 5.11(A)), which allows us to respond to the possible limitation evoked in relation to a confusion between figures and elements of the map background (see Figure 5.6, right). Here, the combined representation avoids a degraded perception of the figures, which are superimposed on shaded areas, as shown when color is absent (Figure 5.11(B)). We also note that this representation allows us to visually see that the different fragments of the PLZ do not all have the same level of probability (see the fragment located in the upper left part of Figure 5.11(A) as opposed to the largest fragment in the center of the figure) and/or that a fragment does not have a homogeneous probability throughout its extent. For example, the area in the center and at the top of the largest fragment has the largest figures (and the most pronounced red background), reflecting the highest probability of the victim's presence.

– On the previous display, and at the request of the rescuer, by adding the contours of the three CLZs that were used to calculate the PLZ (see Figure 5.12), which helps explain to the rescuer the role played by each clue.

These different representations can thus contribute to visually supporting the reasoning operated by the rescuer and guiding their verbal interactions with the requester by taking the information transcribed on the map into account. Finally, as this alert actually took place in the past, our partner from the Peloton de Gendarmerie de Haute Montagne (PGHM) was able to provide us with the exact location of the victim after we processed the case example. Figure 5.13 shows his position, which we can see is well included in the PLZ that we calculated from the clues.

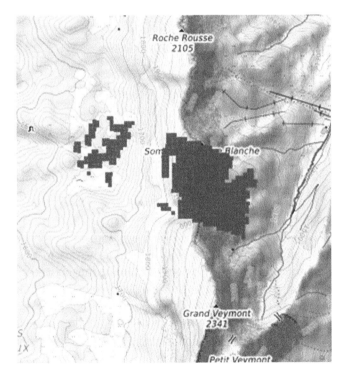

Figure 5.10. *PLZ display – overview: OpenTopoMap map background (OpenStreetMap contributors, SRTM). For a color version of this figure, see www.iste.co.uk/pinet/geographic2.zip*

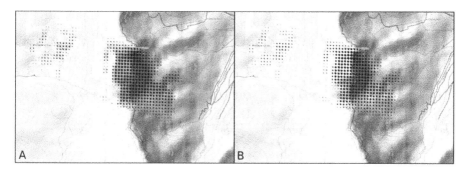

Figure 5.11. *Display of the main fragment of the PLZ using the proportional circles technique, (A) with red gradient background and (B) alone: OpenTopoMap map background (OpenStreetMap contributors, SRTM). For a color version of this figure, see www.iste.co.uk/pinet/geographic2.zip*

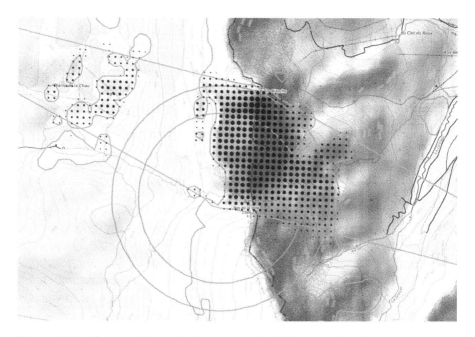

Figure 5.12. *Display of the main fragment of the PLZ, as well as the contours of the three CLZs that allowed its creation: OpenTopoMap map background (OpenStreetMap contributors, SRTM). For a color version of this figure, see www.iste.co.uk/pinet/geographic2.zip*

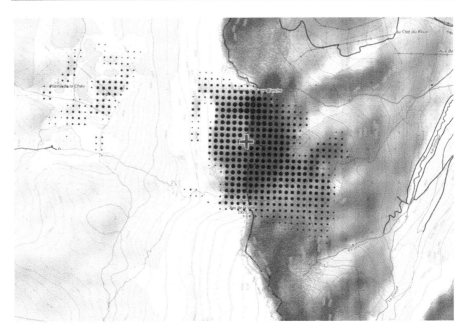

Figure 5.13. *Representation of the victim's position for the Grand Veymont Alert, revealed by the PGHM after the treatment of the alert using our approach: OpenTopoMap map background (OpenStreetMap contributors, SRTM). For a color version of this figure, see www.iste.co.uk/pinet/geographic2.zip*

5.6. Conclusion and perspectives

In the particular framework of the ANR CHOUCAS project and the assistance to the localization of victims in the mountains, in this chapter we have endeavored to illustrate an approach dealing with the question of uncertainty at different levels: the modeling of imprecise locational information, the treatment in a spatialization process of the information and the cartographic restitution of the user to support their reasoning toward the handled problem. The presented works testify moreover to a successful experience of interconnection of two prototypes, GASPAR and RUITOR, dedicated to the input of imprecise locational information and visual restitution (GASPAR) and spatialization (RUITOR), with this interconnection relying on the developed ontologies.

One of our next realizations will consist, for clues relying on some locational relations, of contextually modulating imprecision (fuzzifier), rather than introducing uncertainty on the clue as a whole. Thus, for example, distance expressions ("I am 800 m away", or "I am 2 km away") would be translated with a different margin (800 m plus or minus 400 m, versus 2 km plus or minus 1 km) to consider an uncertainty more adapted to the situation. This may of course also depend on the reference objects or the spatialization relationship composing the clue. This evolution of the tool will be based on the work related to the parameterization of the spatialization methods (fuzzifier in particular) proposed in [BUN 21a], which will be addressed by adapted acquisition components of which a first version has been introduced in [VIR 20]. In order to better take the imprecision of certain reference objects (a valley, a mountain range, etc.) which are intrinsically fuzzy into account, our objective is to extend the method in order to work with reference objects represented in a fuzzy form [BLO 96].

The regular exchanges that we had with a member of the PGHM throughout the project made our approach part of a logic of co-construction of proposals that make us confident about their interest for first aiders. However, beyond the positive feedback on these developments from some of them, it seems essential to us to proceed to more in-depth evaluations. In this objective, we are currently working on the definition of various experimental protocols aiming at validating the different contributions proposed on the level of the graphic restitution of uncertain zones. For example, we will objectively test the contribution of the representation combining figures of proportional size and background color for the perception and interpretation of PLZs. Another experiment considered concerns the study of the advantages for the rescuer of being able to access a 3D view on which the representations of the CLZs and PLZs are mapped (not presented in this chapter, but described in [VIR 22]).

5.7. References

[BAT 19] BATTON-HUBERT M., PINET F., "Formalisms and representations of imperfect geographic objects", in BATTON-HUBERT M., DESJARDIN E., PINET F. (eds), *Geographic Data Imperfection 1: From Theory to Applications*, ISTE Ltd, London, and John Wiley & Sons, New York, 2019.

[BLO 96] BLOCH I., "Fuzzy relative position between objects in images: A morphological approach", *Proceedings of the 3rd IEEE International Conference on Image Processing*, vol. 2, pp. 987–990, 1996.

[BUN 19] BUNEL M., OLTEANU-RAIMOND A.-M., DUCHÊNE C., "Objets et relations spatiales composites et prise en compte du vague pour interpréter un référencement spatial indirect", *Revue internationale de géomatique*, vol. 29, no. 1, pp. 81–106, 2019.

[BUN 21a] BUNEL M., Modélisation et raisonnement spatial flou pour l'aide à la localisation de victimes en montagne, PhD Thesis, Université Gustave Eiffel, Paris, 2021.

[BUN 21b] BUNEL M., "Un état de l'art sur l'imprécision spatiale et sa modélisation", *Cybergeo: European Journal of Geography*, document 966, doi: doi.org/10.4000/cybergeo.36126, 2021.

[FOL 19] FOLLIN J.-M., GIRRES J.-F., OLTEANU-RAIMOND A.-M., et al., "The origins of imperfection in geographic data", in BATTON-HUBERT M., DESJARDIN E., PINET F. (eds), *Geographic Data Imperfection 1: From Theory to Applications*, ISTE Ltd, London, and John Wiley & Sons, New York, 2019.

[FRA 92] FRANK A.U., "Qualitative spatial reasoning about distances and directions in geographic space", *Journal of Visual Languages & Computing*, vol. 3, pp. 343–371, 1992.

[GAI 19] GAIO M., MONCLA L., "Geoparsing and geocoding places in a dynamic space context: The case of hiking descriptions", in AURNAGUE M., STOSIC D. (eds), *The Semantics of Dynamic Space in French: Descriptive, Experimental and Formal Studies on Motion Expression, Human Cognitive Processing*, John Benjamins Publishing Company, Amsterdam, 2019.

[GEN 21] GENDNER V., VAN DAMME M.-D., OLTEANU-RAIMOND A.-M., "Modelling and building of a graph database of multi-source landmarks to help emergency mountain rescuers", *Abstracts of the International Cartographic Association*, vol. 3, pp. 1–2, 2021.

[HAL 18] HALILALI M.S., GOUARDÈRES E., DEVIN F., et al., "Plateforme logicielle pour l'intégration et la composition de services géospatiaux", *Sagéo'2018*, Montpellier, 2018.

[HOP 07] HOPE S., HUNTER G.J., "Testing the effects of positional uncertainty on spatial decision-making", *International Journal of GIS*, vol. 21, no. 6, pp. 645–665, 2007.

[ISO 03] ISO-19112:2003(E), Geographic information – Spatial referencing by geographic identifiers, International Organization for Standardization (TC 211), 2003.

[KOR 19] KORPORAAL M., FABRIKANT S.I., "How are map-based decisions influenced by uncertainty visualization in risky and time-critical situations?", *Abstracts of the ICA*, vol. 1, pp. 1–3, 2019.

[MED 18] MEDAD A., GAIO M., LE NIR Y., et al., "Appariement automatique de données hétérogènes : textes, traces GPS et ressources géographiques", *Sagéo'2018*, 2018.

[OLT 09] OLTEANU-RAIMOND A.-M., MUSTIÈRE S., RUAS A., "Fusion des connaissances pour apparier des données géographiques", *Revue internationale de géomatique*, vol. 19, no. 3, pp. 321–349, 2009.

[OLT 20] OLTEANU-RAIMOND A.-M., BUNEL M., DUCHÊNE C., et al., Ontologies d'objets de repères et de relations de localisation, Livrable L3.2.2 du projet ANR CHOUCAS, IGN, 2020.

[RIV 14] RIVEIRO M., HELLDIN, T., FALKMAN G., et al., "Effects of visualizing uncertainty on decision-making in a target identification scenario", *Computers & Graphics*, vol. 41, pp. 84–98, 2014.

[RUG 16] RUGINSKI I.T., BOONE A.P., PADILLA L.M. et al., "Non-expert interpretations of hurricane forecast uncertainty visualizations", *Spatial Cognition & Computation*, vol. 16, no. 2, pp. 154–172, 2016.

[VAN 19] VAN DAMME M.-D., OLTEANU-RAIMOND A.-M., MÉNEROUX Y., "Potential of crowdsourced data for integrating landmarks and routes for rescue in mountain areas", *International Journal of Cartography*, vol. 5, nos 2–3, pp. 195–213, 2019.

[VIR 19] VIRY M., VILLANOVA-OLIVER M., GAUTIER J. et al., "Improving the search for victims in mountain environments with geovisualization and competing hypotheses management", *ICC'2019*, Tokyo, 15–20 July 2019.

[VIR 20] VIRY M., VILLANOVA-OLIVER M., "Ontologie d'Alerte Choucas : de la modélisation des connaissances à un outil support d'un raisonnement géovisuel", *Geomatica*, vol. 74, no. 3, pp. 87–103, 2020.

[VIR 21] VIRY M., VILLANOVA-OLIVER M., "How to derive a geovisualization from an application data model: An approach based on Semantic Web technologies", *International Journal of Digital Earth*, vol. 14, no. 7, pp. 874–898, 2021.

[VIR 22] VIRY M., "GASPAR – Geoviz application for searching and rescuing people", *Mappemonde*, available at: http://journals.openedition.org/mappemonde/8063, 2022.

[ZAD 65] ZADEH L., "Fuzzy sets", *Information and Control*, vol. 8, no. 3, pp. 338–353, 1965.

[ZAD 78] ZADEH L., "Fuzzy sets as a basis for a theory of possibility", *Fuzzy Sets and Systems*, vol. 28, no. 3, pp. 3–28, 1978.

Uncertainties Related to Real Estate Price Estimation Scales

6.1. Introduction

After having remained inaccessible for a long time [BOU 12], data on land and real estate transactions are now very easily available [CAS 19, JUI 19]. Combined with the development of the online real estate sector [LEF 15, SIT 17], this state of affairs has led to a massive diffusion of real estate price estimates, with many sites now relaying the written press' "prices in your city" [BOU 21]. Thus, whether you are a real estate professional, a private individual in search of a property or a public actor in the process of expropriation, you will be led to use these data to inform yourself about the value of a particular property in a given geographical sector.

Although this immediate access to land and real estate information has many positive aspects, it nevertheless raises fundamental questions: on what methods are price estimates based? Under which conditions are they valid? Few sources provide such information, so much so that we can paradoxically see in the increased accessibility of real estate price estimates a transition between the former "market opacity" (linked to the absence of easily accessible information on real estate markets) and the current

Chapter written by Didier JOSSELIN, Delphine BLANKE, Mathieu COULON, Guilhem BOULAY, Laure CASANOVA ENAULT, Antoine PERIS, Pierre LE BRUN and Thibault LECOURT.

"methodological opacity" (linked to the absence of metadata or precautions for the use of online price references [BOU 21]).

A key methodological issue that needs to be clarified is the geographical dimension of real estate markets: any property is localized and its value is strongly dependent on its environment – and this applies at different scales. However, very often, the estimation of local prices, targeted in time and geographical space, leads to their generalization to other, larger and sometimes vague scales: the *neighborhood*, the *municipality* or the *region,* for example. This unconsidered use of scales, as well as the generalization of estimates from one scale to another, poses a serious problem for the geographer, both from a methodological point of view and from the point of view of the study of changes in the territories: nothing in fact says that the said scales of representation of the real estate markets are the scales at which the latter are really structured. These representations can be cartographic and/or mental, with a strong convergence of the two meanings, since the delimited geographical entity refers to a shared perception of the territory, and, consequently, to a value that is attributed to the assets exchanged in this entity.

Real estate transactions are rather rare in terms of geographic space, because they are not very common locally over short periods of time in metropolitan France (despite an average number of over 1 million per year in recent years). They are a privileged point of entry for studying a number of fundamental phenomena: socioresidential segregation, socioeconomic inequalities in the territories, the impact of public policies on urban fabrics, etc. [LEG 21]. Based on these sources, it is possible to evaluate the potential effect of geographic restitution scale for a statistical estimate of real estate value and to draw recommendations as to the appropriate scales for representing these market movements. Do price references depend on administrative divisions? When real estate transactions are aggregated according to different administrative divisions, do the real estate price references vary? If so, in what way? This is what we propose to study in this chapter using the possibility of estimating prices at different scales and seeking the one that seems most relevant to account for real estate values in their surroundings, independently of a territorial grid imposed on us by data producers or by a particular social demand.

These issues ultimately come back to the problem of *uncertainty*. In the particular case of real estate price estimates, this uncertainty arises from various sources: errors in the data entry itself, the representation of the samples of transactions used to estimate the value of the stock and a lack of knowledge of the statistical and spatial distribution of prices. The first two sources of uncertainty have long been identified and are relatively easy to control. Input errors can be corrected by detecting outliers [KON 06]. Correcting the representation of the sample of transactions can be done by using hedonic methods, which take into account the characteristics of the goods and provide estimates for a "basket of goods" representing the area under study [CAI 19]. On the other hand, the last source of uncertainty, the "statistical-spatial" distribution of prices, is still largely unknown, because it is not often identified. Dealing with the question of the scales of real estate price estimations is therefore a priority issue for research, given that the massive dissemination of cartographic and statistical representations of real estate prices largely interferes with the growing macro-economic weight of real estate [AAL 14].

Thus, we will first emphasize how little the choice of price aggregation scale is taken into account in the representation of real estate markets. Secondly, we will present the methodology for estimating the effect of spatial support on real estate price estimates, using two panels of territorial grids, one administrative and the other functional. Finally, we will present and discuss the results obtained through several scales of real estate price representation.

6.2. The effect of spatial support in real estate price estimation

6.2.1. *The generation of uncertainty in the choice of aggregation scales*

The *Change of Support Problem* (COSP) [KIN 97, KIN 04], defined by Stan Openshaw as the *Modifiable Areal Unit Problem* (MAUP) in geography [OPE 84], results directly from the partitioning of spatial data according to a certain number of elements characterizing the geographical space concerned: number of samples, number of entities per sample and limits of the spatial units of those samples. Potentially, there are an infinite number of spatial divisions whose structure directly impacts the statistical data manipulated. This zoning effect is exacerbated when aggregating the values measured at different levels (the entities of the higher level contain, in most cases, the entities of the lower level). Very concretely, these effects can be observed on the real estate data that we manipulate in two cases: *upscaling* [JOS 19] and *resampling* [LOU 16].

Real estate transaction data are unique in that they are attached to surface entities – parcels – which together form a *partition*. *Stricto sensu*, a partition corresponds to a configuration in which any localized data belongs to a single entity. From a spatial point of view, this means that there is no overlap between entities (spatial subsamples), nor any *holes* in the spatial partition (with the exception of the public domain which is not cadastralized, but on which no real estate transaction for a fee is legally possible). In the first case, *upscaling* consists of aggregating the individual information in the different entities, becoming more and more generalized, which compose the partition at a given scale. The second case refers to situations where the different levels of entities can partially overlap, without perfectly fitting into each other hierarchically. We speak then of *resampling* since each partition corresponds to a new division of the space. In both cases, each scale corresponds to a partition.

Real estate data are likely to fall into both the *upscaling* and *resampling* cases. Real estate transactions are statistical data recorded at the smallest possible scale – the cadastral parcel – and are generally aggregated and made available to the public at larger scales: from the neighborhood to the region, or even the country, by way of the municipality or the urban area. This process of producing statistical information on the real estate market, which is usually always bottom-up, uses two types of grids. The first, based on administrative perimeters, corresponds to a hierarchical structure: cadastral parcels are nested in cadastral sections, which are in turn nested in municipalities, which are nested in cantons, and so on down to regions. The second set of grids, which refers rather to functional and/or actual perimeters, does not correspond to this case. Indeed, while some perimeters overlap (e.g. municipalities in intermunicipal structures), this is not the case for all of them. For example, the EPCIs – Public Establishments of Intercommunity Cooperation – do not aggregate hierarchically (i.e. entirely, as a whole) in the city centers or in the departments. Even if the geographical limits could perfectly well coincide, the municipalities that make them up may belong to different departments. This particular case exists, but remains rare in administrative partitions (e.g. the enclave of the popes in the French department of Vaucluse). The different grids we use here mix these two types of spatial partitioning. This will allow us to evaluate the potential impact of the division, depending on whether it was constructed with an administrative, functional or mixed (administrative and functional) objective.

6.2.2. *Real estate price representation scales rarely questioned*

A utilitarian relationship to supposedly neutral data [DES 01, GIT 13] is becoming widespread with the development of studies on real estate and *propotech* (contraction of "property" and "technology", which groups together the new players and start-ups intending to revolutionize the real estate sector), which can sometimes reduce the production of price references to a quick calculation, thereby concealing the robustness of the indicators, which is sensitive to their scale of aggregation [LOU 16, LEG 21]. Thus, many of the cartographic representations of real estate prices do not really question the choice of a particular scale. There are mainly three modalities for representing real estate markets:

1) Representations of the market by points are, as in the visualization applications of the Demande de Valeurs Foncières (DVF) database, recently made available to all [CAS 19]. In this case, the issue of the aggregation scale does not arise directly, but this does not mean that this choice of representation is good in the absolute, since it fails to simplify the statistical information effectively.

2) Representations at a single scale (often the neighborhood or the municipality, more rarely the EPCI) often are not specifically justified. We can hypothesize that these choices result from two attitudes:

- a "naive" attitude, based on the use of a perimeter known to everyone and which seems to have a certain "evidentiality"; some professionals also create their own partitions by neighborhood, associating to each one a name supposed to be meaningful for their clients;

- a more pragmatic attitude dictated by the availability of other sources of data that can enrich the analysis of transactions; the IRIS (*Îlots Regroupés pour l'Information Statistique*, an infra-communal territorial breakdown proposed by the French institute of statistics INSEE, in force since 1999) is, for example, very frequently used from this point of view, particularly by specialized commercial sites.

3) Finally, some media offer to display prices at different scales, which often correspond to breakdowns that are not explicitly justified and/or imposed by the use of other statistical sources. On many commercial and professional websites, it is possible to view prices at the level of regions, departments, municipalities or IRIS, for example. It is in this approach that this chapter takes position, with a systematic and comparative quantitative measurement across scales, which goes beyond representations that are not explicitly justified.

However, several remarks should be made in addition to this observation. First of all, the scales of representation considered by professionals vary according to the markets and sub-markets in which they operate.

Some of them may thus prefer to represent areas (rural municipalities, small towns) or sub-markets (high-end real estate) with a low number of transactions, for which aggregation would have too distorting an effect. Another example is the preference for administrative divisions (municipalities and, to a lesser extent, EPCIs) in the representation of new housing markets, because of the important role played by local public decision-makers in their operation (drawing up Local Urban Plans (PLU) or PLUI (inter-communal PLUs), validation of building permits, etc.). Like the balancing act between naive and pragmatic attitudes, professionals seem to alternate between commercial criteria and statistical rigor.

Secondly, the arbitrary use of real estate market representation scales is not unique to the press or to professionals in the sector. It is also widespread in scientific publications. Moreover, researchers share certain constraints with professionals in the sector, which are likely to guide their choice of scales. These choices generally arise from the partly contradictory objectives of having, on the one hand, the finest scale and, on the other, the possibility of cross-referencing real estate data with other aggregated databases and/or respecting thresholds for the minimum quantity of sales per spatial unit, notably for reasons of statistical significance or confidentiality. However, the lack of commercial concern leads academics to mobilize certain divisions ignored by professionals, such as the INSEE grid system [BOU 11, LEC 19], which they often consider to be illegible for their clients. However, while this grid does not resolve the issues of sample size variation that impact aggregate statistics, it does have the merit of providing a spatially homogeneous breakdown.

Finally, the unquestioned mobilization of market representation scales does not exclude the existence of a multitude of other methods that take into account the local context of real estate prices. For example, we can mention spatial smoothing methods which, by integrating neighborhood effects, make it possible to reduce the uncertainty linked to the punctual impact of extreme values or the lack of data [LEG 21]. However, these methods do not resolve the effects of the MAUP, because while smoothing gives the impression of some continuity, it is still calculated from aggregated data at questionable scales. Another way to limit uncertainty is to use ad hoc perimeters that aim to maximize the similarity of aggregated entities within larger grid cells [FEU 21]. These methods, which aim to produce relevant grids for market analysis, have been used particularly in studies regarding housing prices, land prices and rents for rental properties [GÉN 19, BRE 20, CAS 22]. Finally, the range of local regression methods can also take into account multi-level price determination. Some applications, for example, mobilize supra-communal ad hoc grids in order to ensure a sufficient sample of transactions, but apply communal fixed effects in order to take into account both scales in the modeling of prices [GÉN 19, BRE 20]. In the same way, recent methodological developments concerning multi-scale geographically weighted multiple regressions (*MGWR*) also make it possible to measure and analyze the spatial variability of the processes influencing real estate prices at different geographical scales [SAC 22].

6.2.3. *Different scales of real estate price structuring*

Markets are structured and segmented at different scales due to the complexity of the spatial contexts that influence price dynamics. At the national level, for example, there are marked differences between regions, largely based on their degree of attractiveness. In particular, productivity [LAF 03] and the tourism function [BUH 06] seem to play a crucial role in structuring prices at this broad scale. These major factors explain, for example, the very high price differentials between the very expensive regions of Île-de-France and Provence Alpes Côte d'Azur and the diagonal of low densities, which has been in demographic and industrial decline for several decades [OLI 16], characterized by particularly low price levels. The geographic targeting of certain public policies also fuels local price differentiation. Tax incentives for rental investment by households, which are inflationary [BON 19], are only accessible in an increasingly small number of municipalities [LEB 22].

At finer scales, infra-regional or departmental, other contextual effects come into play and often determine price gradients: prices decrease as we move away from the Swiss border or from a coastline, or as we move away from large urban areas. Price segmentation can also be observed at the intra-urban level. Price gradients, but also very clear discontinuities, can result from socioresidential segregation. Belonging to a municipality will generate significant price effects, which will be further differentiated at finer scales, as shown, for example, by the traditional price differential between the two banks of the Garonne in Bordeaux. At the intra-urban level as well, urban renewal zones – Concerted Development Zones (ZAC), zones under agreement with the French National Agency for Urban Renewal (ANRU), Priority City Policy Districts (QPV), territorial revitalization operations – have clear effects on local market structures (controlled or lower prices compared to the neighborhood, especially in the case of stigmatized neighborhoods). Finally, the proximity of infrastructure and environmental amenities can also have a positive or negative effect on real estate valuation. The literature on hedonic price modeling has, for example, examined the effect of the proximity of public transport [MAL 09], urban parks [TRA 13], major roads [BRÉ 18] and school catchment areas [FAC 09] on real estate prices. Discontinuity effects in real estate prices can thus sometimes be observed very locally, on the scale of neighborhoods, and even sometimes of streets [GUÉ 09].

In an application context, several scales may be of interest, depending on the problem and the factor influencing price structuring. Whether we are interested in *macro*, *meso* or *micro* levels, we must be able to determine which scale is the most appropriate for studying the level in question. This is the conclusion of several research studies which, since the founding articles by Straszheim and Palm on San Francisco [STR 75, PAL 78], have insisted on the existence of sub-markets within urban spaces, regularly proven since then [WAT 01, BOU 11]. This highlighting of the coexistence of different sub-markets at different scales highlights the theoretical and problematic dimension of the choice of the grid, since it implies that behind the apparent *continuum* of prices in a space hides in fact "a structure of mutual exclusion of hierarchical sub-markets" [TOP 84]. Depending on a chosen grid, which can be considered as "adequate" in a given context and for a given objective, we discretize the price gradients, revealing different spatial structures. We will see that these spatial discretizations induce a non-negligible variability of real estate price estimates.

6.3. Data and indicators for estimating the sensitivity of house prices to the scale of aggregation

6.3.1. *Different territorial grids to test the effects of aggregation*

In order to evaluate the effect of the MAUP from the point of view of *upscaling* and *resampling*, a panel of 10 grid cells is used here, which can be nested (or not, in the case of resampling), one within the other. The experimentation is carried out on the perimeter of the Provence Alpes Côte d'Azur region from 2014 to 2020, in order to have a sufficiently large corpus compatible with bearable computation times, that is, 165,816 real estate transactions concerning houses and 362,249 for apartments. Figure 6.3.1 illustrates the interweaving of administrative divisions, from the parcel to the region, and locates the EPCIs, the population centers and the INSEE IRISs. Figure 6.2 places the 1 km INSEE squares in relation to the administrative entities.

The following is a list of the breakdowns used, from smallest (high sample size) to largest (low sample size):

1) The cadastral parcel is the basic unit of the cadastre. It belongs to the same owner (group of owners) who benefits from real rights on this portion of territory. It may (or may not) support one (or more) dwellings, but it is not necessarily equivalent to the "house" as it is understood in common speech (since our properties may include several parcels, including adjoining ones). For this particular level where, in the notaries' declarations, the same real estate transaction value can be duplicated on several parcels, we have carried out a sorting that eliminates all duplications. At this level, we have 145,144 parcels of houses that have changed ownership (a little more than 7% of the properties have changed ownership several times over the period) and 76,275 parcels concerning apartments (sales may include several apartments, identified by transaction and associated with the same parcel).

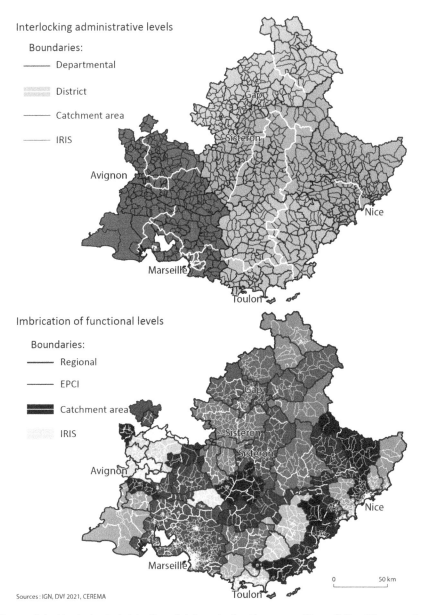

Figure 6.1. *Nested administrative divisions in the Provence Alpes Côte d'Azur region: from the parcel to the region via administrative and/or functional divisions. For a color version of this figure, see www.iste.co.uk/pinet/geographic2.zip*

2) The cadastral section – which exists only in the largest municipalities – groups several cadastral parcels within the same municipality (cadastral parcels, cadastral sections and municipalities thus intermingling). This is a strictly administrative division, which reflects the evolution of land use (new sections are regularly created when a municipality becomes urbanized, for example). For houses and apartments, the parcels are grouped into 11,803 and 7,089 sections, respectively, with apartments being more concentrated in dense urban areas.

3) The 1 km grid (9,645 for transactions concerning houses and 4,470 for apartments) stands out because of its "neutrality" and its arbitrary character, contrary to administrative grids, for example, and thus protects against "biases due to inequalities in the shape and size of the grids" [PUM 97]. However, it is not a solution for the MAUP [BOU 11], due to the variations in the size of the samples in each grid. The relatively smaller number of INSEE grid cells compared to sections is explained, on the one hand, by the fact that isolated scattered houses are not taken into account in the grid cells, and, on the other hand, by the fact that small sections are more frequent in urban areas, where most of the mutations of parcels occur.

4) The IRIS is the basic building block for the dissemination of sub-municipal data. It must respect geographic and demographic criteria and have contours that are unambiguously identifiable and stable over time[1]. It should be noted that not all municipalities are divided into IRIS, but that when they are, they are nested within the municipalities. The number of IRIS aggregating real estate transactions for the two types of housing is quite similar: 2,270 for houses and 2,250 for apartments.

5) The municipality is the smallest of the territorial communities. It is primarily an administrative network, but also corresponds in part to a functional space: despite the sprawl of cities and the generalization of commuting on a supra-communal scale. The municipalities provide essential services to their inhabitants and are identified as relatively homogeneous entities. A total of 951 municipalities are involved for houses and 836 for apartments.

6) The canton is now only an administrative district for the organization of elections. The transactions affect 107 townships for both houses and

---

1 Available at: https://www.insee.fr/fr/metadonnees/definition/c1523/.

apartments. Aggregation to larger and larger grids converges the sample sizes for both housing categories.

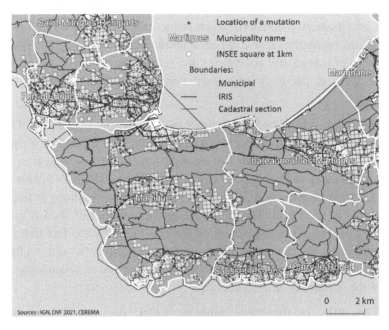

Figure 6.2. *Focus on the Martigues sector: localized mutations, INSEE grids and breakdowns (municipalities, IRIS and cadastral sections). For a color version of this figure, see www.iste.co.uk/pinet/geographic2.zip*

7) The EPCI (Public Establishment of Intercommunal Cooperation) is a grouping of municipalities administering, by delegation, certain competences of the municipalities. The latter fit into the EPCIs, but the EPCIs do not fit into any other structure. Initially conceived by the legislator as a means of matching administrative perimeters with the functional areas of cities, they were eventually frequently formed according to local logics of solidarity and opposition between municipalities polarized by the same center. Since 2017, all the municipalities in France belong to an EPCI. There are 52 in our regional data.

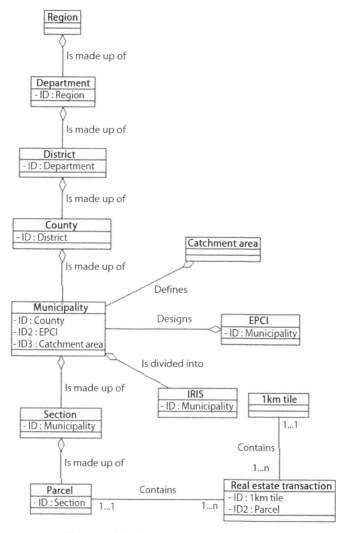

Figure 6.3. *UML diagram presenting the organization of the multi-scale database*

8) The living areas (22 in total in our data) correspond to the "smallest territory in which the inhabitants have access to the most common facilities and services"[2]. They therefore do not overlap with other perimeters.

---

2 Available at: https://www.insee.fr/fr/information/2115016/.

9) The arrondissement (18 in total) is the intermediate administrative level between the canton and the department, corresponding to the area of action of a sub-prefect.

10) The department (6 in the Provence Alpes Côte d'Azur region) is an intermediate territorial authority between the district and the region.

This panel of grids deliberately excludes frequently used grids such as the urban catchment areas or, more generally, all perimeters linked to polarization phenomena. Indeed, the latter have the disadvantage of not covering the entire national territory, or that of the Provence Alpes Côte d'Azur region, and would therefore distort the test of the effect of the change of scale on the price references obtained, since many transactions would slip through the statistics. It should also be noted that the size of the samples of entities is extremely wide (from 11,803 cadastral sections to six departments). This leads to a very large variation in the number of 528,065 transactions (in total for houses and apartments) distributed within the entities of the divisions considered. The UML diagram in Figure 6.3 details the levels of scale and their relationships.

6.3.2. *A national database of geolocalized real estate transactions in France: DVF*

Real estate prices tend to be considered as a spatially continuous variable. This impression is fed by the release of aggregated maps at different levels of scale or by the release of smoothed maps estimating real estate prices on the scale of the entire national territory. However, it is the real estate sales, recorded at different points in the territory, that form the basis for the construction of this variable, which is intrinsically discrete. The spatial distribution of sales is thus characterized by its irregularity across space, its concentration within urban areas and also by its variability over time. Several databases currently list real estate sales and their characteristics. They are all based on the same single source, the notarial deed [CAS 17] and diverge from the point of view of the producer of the data (notaries, General Directorate of Public Finances or DGFIP, private companies), of the structuring of the base, as well as the channel of transmission and the conditions of access to the information. For a long time, two databases coexisted: the one produced by notaries (PERVAL-BIEN) and the one produced by the DGFIP (Land Value Applications or DVF (Figures 6.4 and 6.5)).

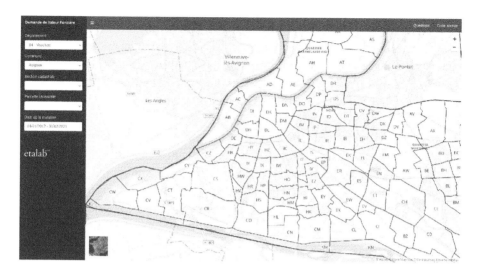

Figure 6.4. *Exploration of cadastral sections of the city of Avignon on the DVF site of Etalab (CEREMA) (https://app.dvf.etalab.gouv.fr/). For a color version of this figure, see www.iste.co.uk/pinet/geographic2.zip*

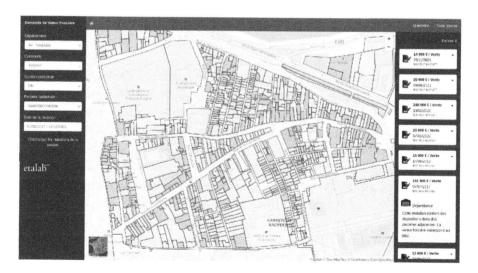

Figure 6.5. *Exploration of the mutated parcels of a cadastral section of the city of Avignon on the DVF site of Etalab (CEREMA): https://app.dvf.etalab.gouv.fr/; on the right: the list of real estate transactions, where the amount (in €) and the date of mutation are mentioned. For a color version of this figure, see www.iste.co.uk/pinet/geographic2.zip*

The opening of DVF to the general public in 2019 has led to a multiplication of versions of this database as well as the development of new databases integrating all or part of these data. The interest for researchers is to now have a disaggregated (the statistical individual being the real estate sale) and geolocalized database, which is exhaustive and available on a national scale (except for Alsace and Moselle departments) since 2014. Thus, the DVF open access database can be used for the entire national territory for the 7 years available (2014–2020). Sales specifically related to the housing market are extracted from the database for each single property in the Provence Alpes Côte d'Azur region. Indeed, in the case of "multiple sales", it is not possible to know the share of the total amount of the sale allocated to each property, which introduces information imperfection (Follin in [BAT 19]).

In order to maximize the significance of the indicators at the finest aggregation grids, that is, to retain the largest number of sales in our sample, the data are filtered on the sole criterion of property type over a 7-year period. Real estate sales are thus segmented into two sub-markets, houses and apartments, which are distinguished both by different price levels and by a differentiated geography (apartments being over-represented in urban centers and houses in suburban areas).

The data preparation work consisted of extracting a complete version of the DVF database and then using a Geographic Information System (PostGIS), via the files themselves for the administrative partitions or by spatial queries for the INSEE grids, to acquire the identifiers of the entities at higher scales. For example, at the root of the process, we must know the respective identifiers of the grid and the parcel in which the real estate transaction occurred, as shown in Figure 6.3. This information must be known up to the fully aggregated partition, which is the region in our case. We thus had to delete some transactions that were poorly geolocated or whose membership vector to the entities of the different partitions was erroneous or incomplete (transaction outside INSEE grids). The duplicated data (concerning the same transactions with identical amounts) were reduced to a single statistical individual, assigned to the first of the associated mutated parcels.

In the remainder of this chapter, we will refer alternately to real estate transactions, land transfers, land values and real estate prices, all of which relate to a price established at the time of the transaction.

6.3.3. *Representation of aggregated statistics in the form of scalograms*

A *scalogram* is a graph that cross-references an aggregated statistical estimator across scales (see Figure 6.8). More precisely, it is a scatterplot where:

– in X, aggregation levels are positioned in descending order of sample size (from the largest sample composed of entities with few values to the smallest sample whose entities contain the most values); in our case, these are territorial division levels;

– in Y, we calculate an estimator of the central value or dispersion of the variable being studied.

Plotting the scalogram shows the evolution of the estimator along the scales, making it possible to compare them and understand their impact on the statistical estimator under study. To create a scalogram, we need to have a complete data file in line with the UML diagram in Figure 6.3, taken from DVFs in the Provence Alpes Côte d'Azur region between 2014 and 2020, for transactions involving houses and apartments. We also need to choose statistical estimators. For central values, we use the mean and median, which will enable us to estimate the price per meter. For dispersion, we choose the standard deviation, which will provide us with dual information on the uncertainty surrounding the price estimate. For the statistical analysis of spatially constrained random permutations, we'll also usebox plots, a rich and synthetic representation of these two central values and the shape of the distribution.

The calculation method consists of a double statistical aggregation according to the scale:

1) At the level of each entity, for a spatial partition at a given scale, we list real estate transactions and apply an indicator (mean, median or standard deviation) to them.

2) For a given partition, we retrieve the list of values calculated for all of the entities in the partition in the first calculation step, and apply to them an indicator that is statistically consistent with the first. Depending on the mathematical norm considered, this leads to the calculation of L_2 as the mean of the means and standard deviations, and L_1, as the median of the medians of

the prices of the entities in the manipulated partition. Figure 6.6 illustrates the calculation method applied in the case of the mean.

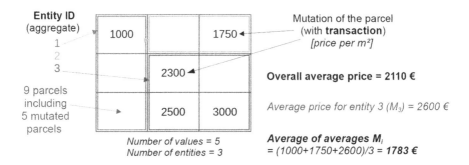

Figure 6.6. *Example of an aggregated statistical theoretical calculation for nine parcels and three entities; it can be seen that the values differ between the overall average of the five prices (€2,110) and the overall average of the prices of the three entities (€1,783). For a color version of this figure, see www.iste.co.uk/pinet/geographic2.zip*

6.4. Methodology for studying variations in real estate price estimates according to scale

6.4.1. *Preliminary methodological considerations*

The first assumption underlying this research is that partitions have a non-negligible influence on the estimation of aggregate prices. We wish to identify this influence, and to know its extent, for the different partitions studied, be they administrative (e.g. section, département), statistical (INSEE grid) or functional (EPCI, catchment area). Essentially, the impact of these divisions lies in the strong link between the statistics used and the samples handled. In particular, the size of the sample is a determining factor in its ability to maintain stability in the estimate. Considering the law of large numbers and the central limit theorem, the larger the sample, the smaller the impact of adding a new element on the variance, as the estimator converges toward the mathematical expectation. In our dual aggregation process, this sample size bias can be observed with:

– prices within each spatial entity;

– aggregate prices in the entities making up each partition.

As the average number of transactions in the entities of a partition increases, the number of entities in that partition decreases. This "balance effect" can be found in analysis of variance (inter vs. intra), but its actual role in relation to COSP or MAUP is unknown, depending on the combined sensitivities of the variances. What we do know is that producing aggregate statistics on small samples involves risks and generates uncertainty. In our case, this risk is omnipresent and acts at both aggregation levels mentioned under the balance effect evoked.

The second assumption is the existence of "relevant" scales, with a certain degree of optimality. If we can compare variations in price estimates between scales, we may be able to determine the most reliable scale for reproducing average and median prices, depending on the problem posed or the structure to be observed. This scale could correspond to the one that is further removed from the aleatory case, that is, the one that maximizes the influence of geographical explanation in the spatial organization of the partition entities under consideration. Indeed, since we are moving away from a homogeneous random distribution, we can think that each aggregate of values (within spatial entities) gives a fairly accurate idea of the local specificity setting an average price level. This approach has been proposed and discussed in previous biodiversity estimation studies [JOS 08]. It requires the implementation of a directed random resampling procedure.

6.4.2. *A random sample generator to eliminate scale uncertainty*

The approach we propose in this article can be broken down into three steps:

– First, we calculate the statistical values for all partitions at all scales, to build the scalogram. This means repeating the operation described in Figure 6.6 for all levels of the geographic scale. This is the observation case.

– In a second step, we perform the same calculation, but this time with random resampling, applying 10,000 permutations of the localized real estate transactions. This calculation is 10,000 times more time consuming and, for our real estate data corpus, requires the use of a relatively powerful server. However, after various empirical tests, we are assured of convergence toward the random case.

– Finally, for a given statistical indicator, we calculate the *relative spread* between the observation and the random event, relative to the random event, which shows how far the observed data (real estate transactions) deviate from a random distribution.

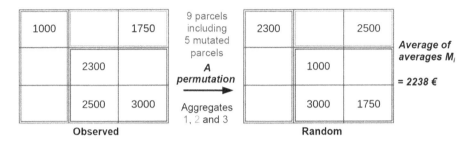

Figure 6.7. *Example of a price permutation constrained by the location of the mutated parcels; we can see that the overall average of the prices of the three entities (€2,238 for this permutation) differs from the overall average of the five prices (€2,110) and from the average of the observed averages (€1,783); this process is repeated 10,000 times to obtain a good representation of the uncertainty. For a color version of this figure, see www.iste.co.uk/pinet/geographic2.zip*

Step 2 of the calculation is illustrated in Figure 6.7: transaction prices are spatially and randomly redistributed across all of the parcels that have actually mutated, and this happens a significant number of times. This amounts to "breaking out" any potential autocorrelated price pools. For example, average price differences, which can be very high when moving from one neighborhood to another, are thus greatly reduced, as the whole converges toward a smoothed average transaction value, independent of the location of the entities considered (cadastral sections, municipality, EPCI, catchment area, as the case may be).

The third and final step, which consists of calculating the relative (normalized) deviation *RD* between the observation (*obs*) and the random case (*random*), is described in the following equation, *S* being the statistic of the average price calculated for a given partition:

$$RD(\%) = 100 * \frac{|S_{obs} - S_{aléa}|}{S_{random}}$$

By subtracting from the statistical estimates S_{obs} of observed transaction prices those obtained by randomly resampling S_{random} of the same data, subject to location constraints, we estimate the deviation (in proportion) of the observed real estate transaction statistics S from the random case. The value of RD is, most of the time, negative for central values, because the estimate of "randomized" values during permutations is higher than that of the observation. In our computation, this is systematically the case for central values, but not for variability, depending on the variable and scale considered. This is why we add an absolute value to quantify the relative (non-algebraic) deviation in the case of a hypothetical distribution of real estate transactions, with no spatial structure or autocorrelation.

6.4.3. *Presentation of analysis elements in the form of a composite graph*

The analysis of the results, presented in detail in the following section, is based on a *composite graph* allowing cross-analysis (see Figure 6.8). The variable studied is the price per meter of the property exchanged during the real estate transaction on the plot that has changed. The graph combines, for a given type of property (house vs. apartment) in the Provence Alpes Côte d'Azur region between 2014 and 2020, a set of four graphs and for a given type of indicator (central value vs. dispersion estimator):

– The lower part of each graph concerns the (actual) **observation** data, where the scalograms of the observed prices of real estate transactions appear, with the medians and averages of the prices for each partition, to which are added the *relative deviation* (*RD*) of the observations to the random case, represented by the surface of the circle.

– The upper part represents the (theoretical) **random case**, providing statistics on indicator variability after 10,000 random redistributions of prices per meter.

Box plots are interpreted in the classic way: the median is represented by a horizontal segment, and the height of the box corresponds to the interquartile range (the length of the range covering 50% of observations, 25% above the box and 25% below). The segments have a length equal to 1.5 times the interquartile range, so that points beyond them can be interpreted as extreme values (outliers) for data that would come from a normal distribution.

Depending on the graph considered, a point corresponds to one of the three types of calculation (average of averages, median of medians or average of standard deviations) per entity for a given random redistribution.

In addition, each *white dot* in the box plot represents the mean calculated for the indicator and scale level considered. The width of the boxes is proportional to the standard deviation of the data: we thus have two distinct measures of dispersion represented on each axis (in width, the standard deviation and in height, the interquartile range).

For scalograms, the size of the dots is proportional to the relative deviation (RD) (multiplied by 100) of the observation from the average of the 10,000 random redistributions per entity. This RD represents the percentage decrease (if negative) or increase (if positive) observed in relation to a completely random distribution of prices on the territory. If it is zero, the observed distribution of transactions is purely random.

6.5. Results: highlighting structural effects linked to territorial units and scale salience

6.5.1. *An analysis of changes in estimates of average and median prices for apartments and houses in the Provence Alpes Côte d'Azur region from 2014 to 2020*

6.5.1.1. *The case of apartments*

Figure 6.8 shows the variations in estimates of average and median prices per meter for apartments. On the one hand, for the calculation of averages with the 10,000 random price redistributions (right-hand column), each average (represented by a white dot) of averages and each median of averages (central segment of the boxes) are practically equal and constant from one scale to the next. This common value is close to the global average calculated at around €3,252 (the global median being lower and equal to €3,064). It is well known that an average of sub-group averages is not generally equal to the overall average (equality being true for equal numbers per sub-group). The observed variability is visualized here by box plots. However, the large number of resamplings carried out implies that the mean and median of these 10,000 averages stabilize toward the overall mean. The random case thus remains "centered" on the global mean, whatever the scale considered.

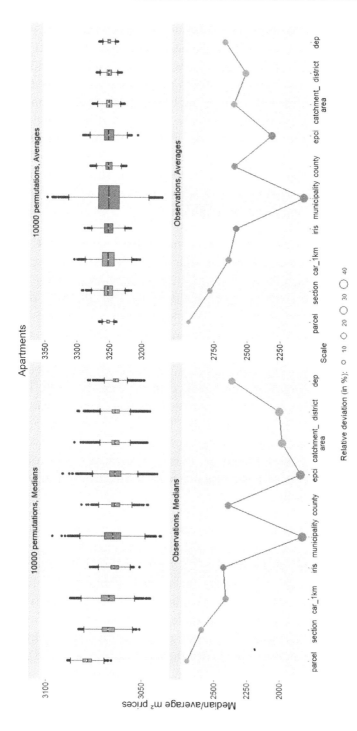

Figure 6.8. *Variations (top) of medians of medians (left) and averages of averages (right) by entity after random redistribution of prices per meter for apartments. Observed values (bottom) for these indicators by scale and circles proportional to the relative spread (%); c.a.: catchment areas. For a color version of this figure, see www.iste.co.uk/pinet/geographic2.zip*

If we now compare the different scales, we can see a symmetry in the dispersion of averages from one scale to the next. Leaving aside the IRIS and cantons, the dispersion of averages increases from the plot to the municipality, then decreases to the department (a phenomenon observed both for standard deviations with the width of the boxes and for the interquartile range with their height). As prices have been redistributed in a completely random way, this highlights the role of scale, with a particularly strong effect for the municipalities where dispersions between the different simulated averages are maximal, which is also true for the median. This scale seems to be the one that generates maximum price variability, both within each entity and across the sample of entities in the partition.

Still on the subject of averages, if we compare the random results with what has actually been observed (bottom right of graph), we first observe a clear difference, with much lower observed averages for each partition and a gap that can exceed 30% for the municipalities. First of all, we have an illustration of Simpson's paradox [SIM 51], since the averages for each entity are lower than the overall average calculated at about €3,252. What is more, their distance from the simulated values in the box plots (representing price distribution independence) highlights the cluster effect (*cluster*). Logically, this effect is less pronounced for small entities (parcels) with fewer transactions than for larger ones. Once again, the behavior of municipalities is singular, as is that of EPCIs in second place. These two breakdowns are the most homogeneous in terms of real transaction values per entity and, at the same time, the most heterogeneous in terms of randomly redistributed property prices. This observation is corroborated by the relative spread, which is maximal for both levels of the scale.

The left-hand column of Figure 6.8 repeats the same calculations, but for medians of median prices. Compared to the graphs obtained for the average, the more stable character of the median is clearly evident, with much less pronounced dispersions. What is more, the median stabilizes toward the overall median (€3,064), starting with partitions of smaller entities (IRIS). For this sturdy indicator, it is also remarkable to note the particular role of municipalities and EPCIs, with the cluster effect clearly marked by the minimum values of median prices per meter, the maximum values of RDs and the pronounced spread of box plots. The relatively similar shape of the observation curves obtained with medians and averages can also be interpreted as the manifestation of the geographical effect, since the results seem to depend only on the scales and not on the metrics employed.

As for the relative spread, it can approach 40% (medians of municipalities, EPCIs). However, for most breakdowns, it remains fairly low, which means that the distribution of transaction values is relatively close to a random distribution, independent of breakdowns. Moreover, median prices at the catchment area and arrondissement levels are more pronounced than their respective averages (median values lower than average values). This reveals an asymmetrical shape in the distribution of prices observed at these two scales (there is a greater number of low price values), which is not found in the two corresponding random distributions (this being due to the "symmetrization" of the distribution induced by the random permutations).

The same composite graph is presented for transactions involving houses in Figure 6.9. The stabilization toward the overall median (€3,100) and the overall average (€3,328) is apparent from the IRIS level upwards for the medians, and for all entities for the average. Furthermore, the symmetry of the shapes of the box plots centered on the municipalities no longer seems to apply: from canton to department, the random distributions resemble each other (their variability does not decrease with aggregation). We can also see that the relative spread is almost nil for small entities (plots and sections, where it even becomes positive for the latter) and very low for IRIS: for these small administrative divisions, we can no longer highlight any cluster effect, as the distribution of prices per meter is virtually random. Overall, for houses, there is less spatial autocorrelation than for apartments, whatever the level of scale considered, with a relative difference divided by two. However, we still note the particular role played by municipalities (and EPCIs for medians).

6.5.2. *Analysis of changes in standard deviation estimates of average prices for apartments and houses in the Provence Alpes Côte d'Azur region from 2014 to 2020*

As mentioned above, it is also interesting to consider the variability of the real estate transaction prices studied in order to qualify the uncertainty associated with price estimates according to a given scale. We do this by calculating the means of the standard deviations of prices for each partition. Figure 6.10 compares apartments (on the left) and houses (on the right), with the same types of statistical representations as above: box plots of the 10,000 standard deviations of average prices per meter and the corresponding scalograms, with relative spreads by scale level.

6.5.2.1. *The case of houses*

In Figure 6.10, the parcels have been eliminated from the graph because the internal variability was not sufficient to be calculated. For this indicator, variability is relatively low for random permutations (generalized collapse of the box plots, except, again, for municipalities). If we set aside the 1 km INSEE squares and the municipalities for the apartments and, to a lesser extent, the EPCIs – which, as it were, "fall off" the curve – we can see that dispersion increases as entities increase in size. Average standard deviations stabilize at the township level, for both apartments and houses (the overall standard deviation for these properties is €1,547 and €1,567 respectively). In the case of the moment of order 2, stabilization by the law of large numbers requires more observations, as the variability becomes of order 4. This constraint makes the estimation of indicators of variability more delicate, as it requires a larger number of observations.

It is also remarkable to observe a relatively similar curve between the 10,000 random permutations and the observed values, which was not the case for the central values (notably the averages, which remained particularly stable across the scales). This shows the decisive impact of spatial support on price variance, a phenomenon that is well known when manipulating indicators of variability (standard deviations, diversity indices such as entropy, for example) [MAH 07, JOS 09]. It is also satisfying to see that standard deviations are significantly lower for observations than for random distributions. This last graph thus highlights the lower variance *intra* within entities, and thus their marked cluster effect. It is worth noting that INSEE squares reveal the lowest standard deviations of both random and observed samples. Their geometric regularity has a clear uncertainty-reducing effect. As for the RD, this time they extend over a narrower range (from around 20–45%), but are overall at higher values.

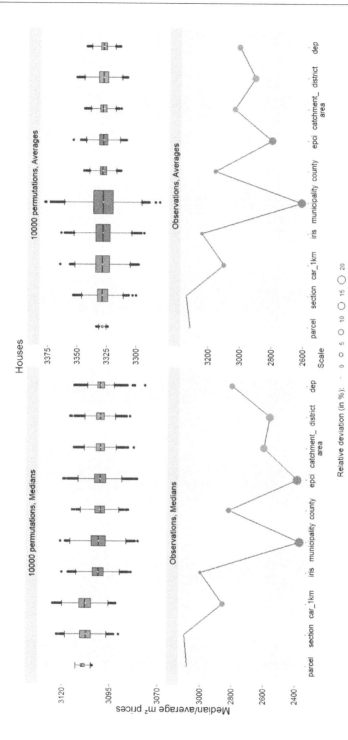

Figure 6.9. *Variations (top) of medians of medians (left) and averages of averages (right) by entity after random redistribution of m prices for houses. Observed values (bottom) for these indicators by scale and circles proportional to the relative spread (%); c.a.: catchment areas. For a color version of this figure, see www.iste.co.uk/pinet/geographic2.zip*

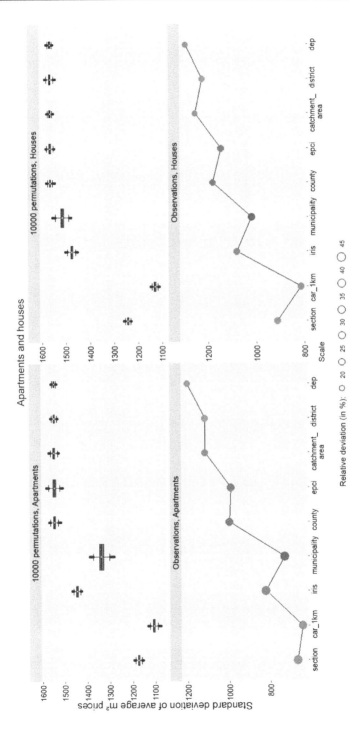

Figure 6.10. *Variations (top) in mean standard deviations for apartments (left) and houses (right) by entity after random redistribution of m prices. Observed values (bottom) for this indicator by scale and property type; c.a.: catchment areas. For a color version of this figure, see www.iste.co.uk/pinet/geographic2.zip*

6.5.3. *Cross-sectional analysis on composite graphs*

6.5.3.1. *The cluster effect of spatial support*

It is interesting to note that the change in property type has little influence on the overall shape of the curves obtained, be it for the series of box plots, for the scalograms, for the central values (price averages and medians), or for their standard deviations. There is thus a certain similarity in the house and apartment transaction data across scales, which is essentially explained by the relationship between the variable under study (prices per meter) and the topological structure of the entities making up the partition at a given scale (location of transactions and shape of partitions). The special cases of municipalities and EPCIs, which exhibit more spatial autocorrelation in real estate prices than the other partitions, should always be noted.

It is also possible to separate the analysis of the two types of indicators of centrality or dispersion of property prices, applied indifferently to apartments or houses. In the case of random sampling, central values show both the greatest stability of values and the greatest variation in estimated price distributions across scales (this is slightly less true in the case of price medians). Exactly the opposite is true of standard deviations, whose estimated values stabilize at the township level, but are highly variable at finer levels. Moreover, central values fluctuate widely across scales (except for 1 km INSEE squares and, to a lesser extent, municipalities and EPCIs), while variance increases steadily from fine scales (section) to more generalized partitions (département), showing the regular impact of spatial support on uncertainty.

Finally, the RD also behaves homogeneously, whether we consider apartments or houses. Its values are high for house price averages and medians (although average and median values are quite low), and lower for price dispersion (standard deviations) (while standard deviation values are higher). Finally, we note the obvious relationship between the relative spread and the dispersion of random samples: the more the random samples generate instability in the distribution of simulated prices, the lower the mean and median observed values, and the higher the RD (in absolute value), showing that observation deviates further from randomness. This indicates a more pronounced clustering effect for spatial partitions whose random permutations have generated more variability, and therefore stronger internal spatial autocorrelation within the entities of these partitions.

6.5.3.2. *Search for the right scale*

In each case, the municipality is the pivotal scale, maximizing the deviation from the random case. This is followed by EPCIs and, to a lesser extent, other breakdowns depending on the statistical metrics used: catchment area and arrondissement for central values, INSEE squares, cadastral sections and IRIS for dispersion. Applying the expectations of our method for eliminating the effect of spatial support, we can affirm that, on the data series relating to property prices per meter in the Provence Alpes Côte d'Azur region from 2014 to 2020, the municipality is the breakdown that concentrates mostly on cluster effect and spatial autocorrelation, for both apartments and houses. The EPCIs, which are made up of them, reproduce this property to a greater or lesser extent. When it comes to estimating property prices, the commune remains the least biased scale, if we consider its local capacity to differentiate property values, especially as it records the highest values of RD, both for central values and for the indicator of price variability – standard deviation. However, the municipal level presents the greatest uncertainty among the partitions, with the least concentrated random distribution of standard deviations in the simulated samples, as well as a high mean value of variability, particularly for houses.

We may think that it is the intermediate position of the municipal scale, allowing a good balance between the size of the price samples within entities and the size of the overall sample of prices aggregated per entity for the whole partition that could induce low variances *intra* and *inter*. This proposition is invalidated by the proximity of the townships, all of whose price values (both observed and random cases) move very quickly away from the points or shapes of the townships' box plots. So it is not just a statistical effect, but the impact of the spatial organization of the transactions observed. This observation is reinforced by the observed reversal in the position of EPCIs, which are much closer to municipalities than to cantons, even though they are direct neighbors in the incremental scaling process. This phenomenon highlights the local logic (similarity and homogeneity of transaction prices within entities) of EPCIs, unlike cantons, which are merely electoral districts.

Finally, we need to assess the confidence we can place in our estimates of average or median property prices per meter. To do so, we have at our disposal not only the distributions (in the form of box plots) and central price values of the 10,000 samples simulating the random case at a given scale, but also the complete series of standard deviations of average prices along the scales. As we have seen, this value increases somewhat mechanically as the aggregation process unfolds. We also know that the more entities (of small size, i.e., containing few real estate transactions) the partition contains, the lower the estimated price variability. Uncertainty increases with the level of scale, which relativizes the existence of a relevant scale by the risk of error tainting, all the more so as the RD values of price standard deviations remain relatively close to one another, for both apartments and houses.

6.6. Conclusion and discussion

Applying the method for assessing statistical variations in real estate prices in relation to scale, and searching for a suitable scale, is of both methodological and thematic interest. From a methodological point of view, the spatial apprehension of real estate transactions implies dealing with relatively rare events whose patterns are highly irregular, combining areas of very high concentration with vast expanses marked by a very low density of data points. From a more thematic point of view, the identification of meaningful scales of representation for the real estate market is all the more important as it occupies a central [SCH 09, AAL 14, PIK 13] and growing place [PIK 13, WET 17, ADK 21] in wealth inequalities. Local market dynamics can reinforce inequalities in the sociospatial distribution of real estate wealth [LEG 21] and the scale of cartographic representation chosen is not neutral in understanding these phenomena [LEC 19].

In this chapter, we have shown that the scale of aggregation has a significant effect on the estimation of average and median property prices, for both apartments and houses. On the one hand, the variability of price estimates is directly impacted by the level of aggregation, in a virtually linear fashion. The higher the level of aggregation, the greater the variability. On the other hand, the difference between observed price values and their random distribution does not exceed 40%. In some cases (cadastral sections, IRIS and, to a lesser extent, 1 km INSEE squares), the price distribution is very close to random, meaning that there is no spatial autocorrelation or cluster effect in property prices. Providing an average value on the basis of these geographical scales, whose distribution of transaction prices is practically random, is not useful: the overall average price value would suffice. On the other hand, averages by municipality or EPCI are very likely to be more accurate, as they take into account local specificities (moving away from the case of random distribution). With the addition of dual information on price uncertainty at these scales, we can retain the municipality which, despite everything, shows a fairly low standard deviation of price averages, despite relatively high variability (for example, compared to the INSEE division by squares). It therefore represents the best compromise. Finally, from a practical point of view, we should bear in mind that the smaller the sample used to calibrate the price, the higher the probability that the value will differ from the mean of the values in this sample.

From a geographical point of view, the relevance of municipalities, and secondly EPCIs, is justified among the 10 proposed partitions (administrative and/or functional). Indeed, these correspond to the levels of the scale where, within entities, observed prices are the most homogeneous, and where their random redistribution consequently generates the greatest variability. These divisions are the result of the gradual construction of functional zonings (experienced and perceived), hence their properties of cluster effect and spatial autocorrelation. Sociospatial segregation, gentrification and localized impoverishment push these areas toward social specification, sometimes in line with political will. These profiles, inherited from local history, partly determine the average property prices in a municipality. Professionals in the field (real estate agencies, notaries) are not exempt from responsibility in this specification, insofar as they advise future sellers or buyers at the municipal level, by assigning to each municipality a number of descriptive adjectives, linked to the estimated value of the property, likely to orientate the choices of sellers or buyers: municipality "of standing", "with a bad reputation", "dormitory", etc. Unfortunately, we do not have this breakdown in this study, but as it is finer than IRIS and less technical than sections, it could make a significant contribution to understanding the spatial distribution of property values.

While the method applied in this chapter can be reused for future studies on the geography of real estate in France, whether in terms of the real estate market or in other fields, we must nevertheless remain vigilant as to the absolute "relevance" of a division:

– The relevance of a given scale is the result of geo-historical processes that can change over time. For example, the introduction of inter-municipal local urban planning schemes (PLUI), replacing municipal PLUs, is likely to reinforce the relevance of the EPCI division in the new housing sub-market.

– A relevant scale in a given context can become a standard of representation. In this respect, the municipal level remains essential, simply because it corresponds to a division of space shared by individuals. Furthermore, the relevance of a representation is determined by the cartographer's objectives: it does not obey the same criteria in the academic sphere as in the private sector, where the commercial objective is to favor scales perceived as relevant by professionals (developers, asset management advisors or investors), themselves based on the preferences attributed to the final purchasers of the goods (households). The relevance of a mesh is therefore also socially situated. In academic circles, the municipal "convention" is more often surpassed (e.g. by supplementing it with an INSEE grid), while private experts continue to favor sub-municipal partitions (neighborhoods, IRIS) or aggregations thereof (EPCI).

– The relevance of a scale, even if it remains context-dependent, can be self-reinforcing, via a "self-fulfilling prophecy" of price estimates by area, since the majority of real estate market intermediaries use price estimation systems based on spatial divisions. The scale on which real estate prices are represented thus plays the role of a market device [MUN 07], guiding actors' reading of phenomena and influencing their behavior in the direction of a validation a posteriori of supposedly relevant divisions [WEB 16]. In fact, the method we have proposed has the ability to adapt to different variables to be estimated along any type of scale series, enabling a locally and thematically adapted search. What is more, it produces a double estimate of the variable being treated: the value and variability of this value (dual information on uncertainty).

Finally, this research on the relationship between scale and property prices raises the question of the place and status of uncertainty in the methodology used [BAT 19] (aggregation of values, change of scale, comparison of observation with the random case). If we define *random* uncertainty as the natural variation inherent in the random phenomenon under study, and *epistemic* uncertainty as a lack of knowledge in a model [SAL 13], we can try to position our approach in relation to these two definitions. In our case, the random generator of permutations models the uncertainty linked to spatial support, while the random uncertainty of real estate prices themselves is estimated by the standard deviations of prices per scale level. As for epistemic uncertainty, this is largely the result of the hidden effect of spatial support. Anyone wishing to estimate the value of a property cannot know, by expertise, the optimal sample to choose for this estimate, let alone the effect of an inappropriate choice of sample on the estimated value. This is the challenge of this research, which aims to reduce both forms of uncertainty, through a detailed graphical and numerical analysis, in particular by calculating the relative spread of the observation to a theoretical random case of transaction distribution devoid of the geography of real estate prices.

6.7. References

[AAL 14] AALBERS M.B., CHRISTOPHERS B., "The housing question under capitalist political economies", *Housing, Theory and Society*, vol. 31, no. 4, pp. 422–428, 2014.

[ADK 21] ADKINS L., COOPER M., KONINGS M., "Class in the 21st century: Asset inflation and the new logic of inequality", *Environment and Planning A: Economy and Space*, vol. 53, no. 3, pp. 548–572, 2021.

[BAT 19] BATTON-HUBERT M., DESJARDIN E., PINET F. (eds), *Geographic Data Imperfection 1: From Theory to Applications*, ISTE Ltd, London, and John Wiley & Sons, New York, 2019.

[BON 19] BONO P.-H., TRANNOY A., "The impact of the 'Scellier' income tax relief on building land prices in France", *Economie et statistique/Economics and Statistics*, nos 507–508, pp. 91–114, 2019.

[BOU 11] BOULAY G., Le prix de la ville. Le marché immobilier à usage résidentiel dans l'aire urbaine de Marseille-Aix-en-Provence (1990–2010), PhD Thesis, Université de Provence Aix-Marseille 1, Marseille, 2011.

[BOU 12] BOULAY G., BUHOT C., FOURNIER J.-L., "Les chercheurs exclus de l'open data ? Appel à signatures lancé à la communauté de la recherche", *Cybergeo: European Journal of Geography*, available at: http://journals.openedition.org/cybergeo/25520, 2012.

[BOU 21] BOULAY G., BLANKE D., CASANOVA ENAULT L., GRANIÉ A., "Moving from market opacity to methodological opacity: Are web data good enough for French property market monitoring?", *The Professional Geographer*, vol. 73, no. 1, pp. 115–130, 2021.

[BRÉ 18] BRÉCARD D., LE BOENNEC R., SALLADARRÉ F., "Accessibilité, pollution locale et prix du logement : le cas de Nantes Métropole, France", *Economie et statistique*, vols. 500–502, pp. 97–115, 2018.

[BRE 20] BREUILLÉ M., GRIVAULT C., LE GALLO J., Les indicateurs de loyers dans le parc locatif privé. Note méthodologique, Report, Ministère chargé du logement, December 2020.

[BUH 06] BUHOT C., Marché du logement et division sociale de l'espace dans les îles du Ponant, PhD Thesis, Université de Bretagne Occidentale, Brest, 2006.

[CAI 19] CAILLY C., CÔTE J.-F., DAVID A. et al., "Les indices Notaires-Insee des prix des logements anciens Méthodologie v4", *INSEE*, no. 132, 2019.

[CAS 17] CASANOVA ENAULT L., BOULAY G., GÉRARD Y., et al., "Deux bases de données, aucune référence de prix", *Revue d'économie regionale urbaine*, no. 4, pp. 711–732, 2017.

[CAS 19] CASANOVA ENAULT L., BOULAY G., COULON M., "Une aubaine pour les géographes ? Intérêts des fichiers open DVF sur les transactions foncières et immobilières et précautions d'usage", *Cybergeo: European Journal of Geography*, available at: http://journals.openedition.org/cybergeo/33602, 2019.

[CAS 22] CASANOVA ENAULT L., PERIS A., "L'articulation des prix fonciers et immobiliers en France : une géographie des marchés locaux", *Foncier en débat*, available at: https://fonciers-en-debat.com/larticulation-des-prix-fonciers-et-immobiliers-en-france-une-geographie-des-marches-locaux/, 2022.

[DES 01] DESROSIÈRES A., "Entre réalisme métrologique et conventions d'équivalence : les ambiguïtés de la sociologie quantitative", *Genèses*, no. 2, pp. 112–127, 2001.

[FAC 09] FACK G., GRENET J., "Sectorisation des collèges et prix des logements à Paris", *Actes de la recherche en sciences sociales*, vol. 180, no. 5, pp. 44–62, 2009.

[FEU 21] FEUILLET T., Les effets de contexte en géographie. Des fondements théoriques à la modélisation statistique, Habilitation à diriger des recherches, Université Lyon 3 Jean Moulin, Lyon, 2021.

[GÉN 19] GÉNÉRAL AU DÉVELOPPEMENT DURABLE, Une nouvelle grille de lecture des territoires pour le logement, la maille habitat, Report, Ministère de la Transition écologique et de la cohésion des territoires, 2019.

[GIT 13] GITELMAN L., *Raw Data is an Oxymoron*, Massachusetts Institute of Technology Press, Cambridge, MA, 2013.

[GUÉ 09] GUÉROIS M., LE GOIX R., "La dynamique spatio-temporelle des prix immobiliers à différentes échelles : le cas des appartements anciens à Paris (1990–2003)", *Cybergeo: European Journal of Geography*, available at: http://journals.openedition.org/cybergeo/22644, 2009.

[JOS 08] JOSSELIN D., MAHFOUD I., FADY B., "Impact of a change of support on the assessment of biodiversity with Shannon entropy", *Spatial Data Handling, SDH "2008"*, Montpellier, June 23–25, 2008.

[JOS 09] JOSSELIN D., MAHFOUD I., FADY B., "Analyse exploratoire des effets de support spatial et de robustesse statistique sur la fiabilité de la mesure de la (bio)diversité", *Photo-interprétation/European Journal of Applied Remote Sensing*, vol. 45, pp. 3–11 and pp. 35–41, 2009.

[JOS 19] JOSSELIN D., MAHFOUD I., FADY B., "Impact of the scale on several metrics used in geographical object-based image analysis: Does GEOBIA mitigate the modifiable areal unit problem (MAUP)?", *ISPRS International Journal of Geo-Information*, vol. 8, no. 3, p. 156, 2019.

[JUI 19] JUILLARD C., "Le tournant numérique des données immobilières : permanences et recompositions", 2019.

[KIN 97] KING G., *A Solution to the Ecological Inference Problem. Reconstructing Individual Behaviour from Aggregate Data*, Princeton University Press, Princeton, NJ, 1997.

[KIN 04] KING G., ROSEN O., TANNER A. M. (eds), *Ecological Inference. New Methodological Strategies*, Cambridge University Press, Cambridge, 2004.

[KON 06] KONTRIMAS V., VERIKAS A., "Tracking of doubtful real estate transactions by outlier detection methods: A comparative study", *Information Technology and Control*, vol. 35, no. 2, 2006.

[LAF 03] LAFERRÈRE A., DUBUJET F., "Niveau et évolution des prix des logements anciens en province", *Données urbaines*, vol. 4, pp. 293–306, 2003.

[LEB 22] LE BRUN P., "L'État dans la régulation locale : le cas des aides fiscales à l'investissement locatif des ménages en France", *Revue d'économie régionale & urbaine*, pp. 827–841, available at: https://www.cairn.info/ revue-d-economie-regionale-et-urbaine-2022-5-page-827.html, 2022.

[LEC 19] LE CORRE T., Paris à tous prix. Analyse des inégalités par une géographie de l'investissement sur le marché immobilier résidentiel en Île-de-France, PhD Thesis, Université Paris 1-Panthéon Sorbonne, Paris, 2019.

[LEF 15] LEFEBVRE T., Une nouvelle ère pour l'intermédiation en immobilier résidentiel : fondements, digitalisation et limites, PhD Thesis on Management Sciences, Université Paris Dauphine, Paris, 2015.

[LEG 21] LE GOIX R., CASANOVA ENAULT L., BONNEVAL L. et al., "Housing (in) equity and the spatial dynamics of homeownership in France: A research agenda", *Tijdschrift voor economische en sociale geografie*, vol. 112, no. 1, pp. 62–80, 2021.

[LOU 16] LOUVET R., JOSSELIN D., GENRE-GRANDPIERRE C., et al., "Impact des niveaux d'échelle sur l'étude des feux de forêts du sud-est de la France", *Revue internationale de géomatique*, vol. 26, no. 4, pp. 445–466, 2016.

[MAH 07] MAHFOUD I., JOSSELIN D., FADY B., "Sensibilité des indices de diversité à l'agrégation", *Revue internationale de géomatique*, vols. 3–4, pp. 293–308, 2007.

[MAL 09] MALLE R., "Méthode hédonique et loyers des bureaux en Île-de-France", *Revue d'économie régionale & urbaine*, vol. décembre, no. 5, pp. 905–933, 2009.

[MUN 07] MUNIESA F., MILLO Y., CALLON M., "An introduction to market devices", *The Sociological Review*, vol. 55, no. 2, pp. 1–12, 2007.

[OLI 16] OLIVEAU S., DOIGNON Y., "La diagonale se vide ? Analyse spatiale exploratoire des décroissances démographiques en France métropolitaine depuis 50 ans", *Cybergeo: European Journal of Geography*, available at: http://journals. openedition.org/cybergeo/27439, 2016.

[OPE 84] OPENSHAW S., *The Modifiable Areal Unit Problem*, Geo Books, Norwich, 1984.

[PAL 78] PALM R., "Spatial segmentation of the urban housing market", *Economic Geography*, vol. 54, no. 3, pp. 210–221, 1978.

[PIK 13] PIKETTY T., *Le capital au XXIe siècle*, Le Seuil, Paris, 2013.

[PUM 97] PUMAIN D., SAINT-JULIEN T., *L'analyse spatiale. Localisations dans l'espace*, Armand Colin, Paris, 1997.

[SAC 22] SACHDEVA M., FOTHERINGHAM S., LI Z., "Do places have value?: Quantifying the intrinsic value of housing neighborhoods using MGWR", *Journal of Housing Research*, vol. 31, no. 1, pp. 24–52, 2022.

[SAL 13] SALLAK M., AGUIRRE F., SCHON W., "Incertitudes aléatoires et épistémiques, comment les distinguer et les manipuler dans les études de fiabilité ?", *QUALITA2013*, Compiègne, 2013.

[SCH 09] SCHWARTZ H.M., SEABROOKE L., "Varieties of residential capitalism in the international political economy: Old welfare states and the new politics of housing", in SCHWARTZ H.M., SEABROOKE L. (eds), *The Politics of Housing Booms and Busts*, Palgrave Macmillan, London, available at: https://link.springer.com/chapter/10.1057/9780230280441_1, 2009.

[SIM 51] SIMPSON E., "The interpretation of interaction in contingency tables", *Journal of the Royal Statistical Society – Series B (Methodological)*, vol. 13, no. 2, pp. 238–241, 1951.

[SIT 17] SITTLER P., "Digitalization in real estate", *24th Annual European Real Estate Society Conference*, ERES, Delft, 2017.

[STR 75] STRASZHEIM M.R., *An Econometric Analysis of the Urban Housing Market*, National Bureau of Economic Research, New York, 1975.

[TOP 84] TOPALOV C., *Le Profit, la rente et la ville : éléments de théorie*, Economica, Paris, 1984.

[TRA 13] TRAVERS M., APPERE G., LARUE S., "Évaluation des aménités urbaines par la méthode des prix hédoniques : une application au cas de la ville d'Angers", *Économie et Statistique*, vol. 460, no. 1, pp. 145–163, 2013.

[WAT 01] WATKINS C.A., "The definition and identification of housing submarkets", *Environment and Planning A*, vol. 33, no. 12, pp. 2235–2253, 2001.

[WEB 16] WEBER R., "Performing property cycles", *Journal of Cultural Economy*, vol. 9, no. 6, pp. 587–603, 2016.

[WET 17] WETZSTEIN S., "The global urban housing affordability crisis", *Urban Studies*, vol. 54, no. 14, pp. 3159–3177, 2017.

Representing Urban Space for the Visually Impaired

7.1. Introduction

The ability to move around without hindrance or complication is a right that is not always accessible to everyone. Accessibility of roads and public spaces is a central issue in most countries around the world. In France, the first steps in the government's agenda on this subject go back to the Orientation Law of June 30, 1975. In practice, getting around in urban spaces for people with visual impairments is often a challenge, requiring a long apprenticeship, provided by professionals: locomotion instructors or *orientation and mobility instructors* in North American countries. Indeed, while sighted people acquire the skills they need to get around town from an early age thanks to their environment, those with visual impairments rarely have people around them who are competent to understand the issues and challenges associated with their orientation, mobility, navigation and locomotion [RAT 19].

An essential stage in this autonomy of movement is the ability to construct a mental map of the space traveled through. Two representational frameworks can be used for this mental construction [LON 97]: the *egocentric* representation, where the individual localizes and structures their environment in relation to their position and orientation, and the *allocentric* representation, where the individual constructs their understanding of the

Chapter written by Lisa DENIS, Jérémy KALSRON and Jean-Marie FAVREAU.

environment from an independent reference point. While the egocentric representation is more easily accessible at first glance, the construction of an allocentric representation opens up new possibilities for the use of places: taking a detour, finding a shortcut and reorienting ourselves when lost.

Generally speaking, these constructions are a challenge for people with visual impairments, who must develop this understanding of space and understand their location by massively soliciting memory in addition to sensory feedback: sometimes using low vision, mainly hearing and touch, but also proprioception or even smell [THI 97]. The urban environment is sometimes an asset, and sometimes a hindrance to the perception of the elements needed for this construction, which involves identifying the landmarks essential to localization [BAL 12].

Access to cartographic representations is naturally an essential tool in this construction of space, offering a means of spatializing the various landmarks. Unfortunately, while the democratization of maps for the general public is undeniable, the manufacture of maps for people with visual impairments is still today an underdeveloped activity, essentially a small-scale operation, which lacks design aids [TOU 19a].

In this chapter, we propose to explore the different types of landmarks that can be used by the visually impaired by looking at how to model the degrees of reliability that can be attributed to them. The construction of an ontology dedicated to their description enables us to propose a methodology for designing embossed and multimodal maps in line with users' needs and capabilities. Finally, in the third section, we present a proposal for integrating the uncertainty of location and representation of these landmarks into a textual description, built with a view to being integrated into an interactive 3D map.

7.2. Landmarks as tools for moving around and finding your location

The ability to find your position and move around in urban space, whether based on a mental map offering an allocentric representation, or articulated around fixed pathways via an egocentric representation, requires the identification of geographical markers or *landmarks* with properties adapted to this use. This notion can be found both in the literature [STA 07], and in the tools passed on by locomotion instructors to those with visual impairments [RAT 19]. If you are planning to convey a particular itinerary to another person, either orally or on a map, it is essential to identify the landmarks that can be used by the person reading the description.

However, to the best of our knowledge, there are no works in the literature that propose a way of classifying or selecting the possible landmarks that make up the urban space for use by the visually impaired. In this chapter, we therefore propose to rely on a needs survey conducted during 2021 to identify the needs of the people concerned, and to produce a functional model.

So in May 2021, we produced and distributed a questionnaire for locomotion instructors to get as comprehensive a view as possible concerning how these professionals work with the people they support on the notion of landmarks and how the latter appropriate them. We also conducted four semi-structured interviews with those with visual impairments, asking them about their orientation and mobility practices. In particular, we asked them to describe a route of their choice, and to explain it to another person with a visual impairment.

In the rest of this section, we begin by presenting an analysis of the various terms and concepts that emerged from the questionnaire and comparing it with the literature in the field. We then propose an ontology-based modeling of the different properties and categories of landmarks, integrating the dimension of uncertainty that naturally emerges. Finally, we will test this model on the four itineraries proposed by the people concerned through the prism of the concepts formalized in the first section.

7.2.1. *Gathering needs and uses*

The survey for locomotion instructors contained a total of 55 responses, collected using the Qualtrics software. Only 35 responses were usable, of which 29 were complete. When processing these data, we chose to keep all answers to questions open-ended, even when the participant had not answered all of the questions. Nearly half the participants (13 out of 29) said they had been locomotion instructors for between 10 and 20 years, and more than half said they accompanied blind (21 out of 29) or partially sighted (25 out of 29) pupils several times a week.

The first open question for which we collected responses concerned the definition of landmarks. The qualifiers most cited by participants for a blind user were as follows: reliable (22), permanent (22), distinctive (17), sound/auditory (13), tactile/podotactile (11), kinesthetic (7), detectable (3) and olfactory (2). In this description, we find the three properties that [STA 07] identify as essential: the persistence (or *permanence*) through time of the landmark, the fact that it is perceptibly salient, (*reliable*) to the solicitable senses of (*hearing, (podo)touch, kinesthetics, olfactory*), and the fact that it is informative, (*distinctive*), which several participants explained as "unique to the setting". This main categorization is further reflected in the usage of locomotion instructors, who often use the acronym *PDR* to designate a permanent, distinctive and reliable landmark.

These characteristics are naturally complemented by visual indicators in the responses to the question about visually impaired people: visual (20), contrast (8), size (3) and light/illumination (4).

We also asked participants about the universality of landmarks. The responses were not unanimous on this point, but we did note that tactile information (warning strips, tactile contrasts on the ground) and sound (traffic noise, beacons) were frequently mentioned in the positive responses.

Two questions then asked participants about their knowledge of categorizing landmarks encountered in the literature: landmarks of *decision* versus landmarks of *confirmation* [DOW 77] and the notion of *clues* (translating the notion of *information point* into practice [RAT 19, LON 97]). Around 25% of participants said they were familiar with the first categorization, while 35% were familiar with the second. While the examples of decision and confirmation landmarks proposed by the participants correspond to the usages given in the literature, the notion of landmarks is not used as formally as that of information points [LON 97]. Indeed, while the authors of the article present these points as "although not unique along the path and therefore cannot be considered landmarks, [they] can be in conjunction with other features to provide information about a person's location", several survey participants illustrate the notion of a clue with landmarks that are said to have degraded reliability. Long and Hill [LON 97] propose to call these landmarks *secondary landmarks*, as opposed to *primary landmarks*, which are PDR according to the name in use. Figure 7.1 provides a schematic illustration of this classification.

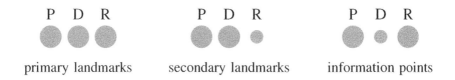

primary landmarks   secondary landmarks   information points

Figure 7.1. *Synthetic representation of the classification of clues [LON 97] according to degree of permanence (P), distinctiveness (D) and reliability (R): total (●) or gradient (◦). For a color version of this figure, see www.iste.co.uk/pinet/ geographic2.zip*

Beyond these different categories, which are fairly similar to those identified in the literature, the answers to the open-ended questions in the survey revealed a number of complementary notions associated with landmarks:

– *surpassing landmark* (seven occurrences): located after an undetectable decision point, for example, a tree along a path after a crosswalk with no kerb or warning strip;

– *anticipatory landmark* (four occurrences): located before a decision point, for example, a waste container along a path just before a crosswalk;

– *combined landmark* (one occurrence): referring to a set of clues that lead to a proof of location, for example, the gate of a private house followed by a hedge whose combination is significantly different from neighborhood fences;

– *conditional landmark* (1 occurrence): a landmark whose reliability is guaranteed if a particular behavior is followed, for example, a post office letterbox that can only be detected by following the wall.

7.2.2. *Modeling landmarks and their uses*

The results of our survey provide the basis for a functional categorization of the landmarks used by people with visual impairments for orientation and mobility. Moreover, they invite us to integrate into this modeling a fine-grained categorization of the uncertainty associated with these landmarks.

While an element of the physical world can be an operational landmark for a visually impaired person, the importance that this person attaches to this element for their orientation and mobility depends on different criteria, each of which offers greater or lesser degrees of reliability. Like the taxonomies used to model uncertainty in geography [DEV 19], we will look at the question of reliance on these elements from different angles.

7.2.2.1. *The detectability of geographical objects*

The first observation we can make about PDR characterization is that two of its components are dedicated to describing the fact that this geographic object is detected (permanent and reliable), while the second component (distinctive) will enable it to be used differently, depending on whether or not it is unique to the context.

As the permanence of a geographic object and the reliability of its detection are not binary, a classic modeling approach is to use a fuzzy measure of these events, that is, to model them by a probability. However, the quantitative estimation of a probability of permanence or reliability is rarely a pragmatic approach, especially when these fuzzy measures can be estimated from collaborative data such as OpenStreetMap (OSM). Devillers et al. [DEV 19] offer several taxonomies for describing uncertainty using a linguistic approach. This is also the approach adopted by the OSM community, which proposes, for example, to describe the vigilance warning strips (BEV) present at the entrances and exits of crosswalks using dedicated semantics[1]. In what follows, we propose to use a decomposition of the probability of an event into five terms: *nul* (0), *low* (0.25), *moderate* (0.5), *high* (0.75) and *total* (1).

In this work, we seek to qualify the various geographical objects in order to decide whether or not to present them on an interactive map (section 7.3). As such a map is intended for several readers, and may include indications to help locate objects (such as their relative position with respect to the path), permanence and reliability cannot be modeled in the same way: permanence is independent of the user's will, and cannot be compensated for by data included in the map (e.g. presence or absence of a terrace along the route), whereas reliability can be increased if the user chooses to devote their attention and time to it (e.g. in the case of the conditional landmarks mentioned in the survey responses). Considering this difference in usage, we propose to model the probability of detecting a landmark by a fuzzy number.

---

1 Available at: https://wiki.openstreetmap.org/wiki/Key:tactilepaving: *yes*,   *incorrect*, *contrasted*, *primitive*, *no*.

Its support is defined by a maximum bound following permanence, and a minimum bound produced by permanence and reliability. This model thus illustrates the range of possible amplitudes depending on the degree of additional information and attention that the user can convoke in locating this geographical object. Figure 7.2 shows some fuzzy numbers combining permanence and reliability modeled by the fuzzy semantics proposed above to describe the probability of detecting a landmark.

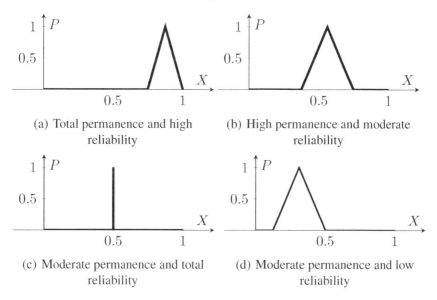

(a) Total permanence and high reliability

(b) High permanence and moderate reliability

(c) Moderate permanence and total reliability

(d) Moderate permanence and low reliability

Figure 7.2. *Examples of fuzzy numbers describing the probability of detecting a geographic object*

7.2.2.2. *Inferring categories of geographical objects*

One of the motivations for this work is to propose a method of data selection and choice of representation with a view to producing a tactile and interactive map for the visually impaired (section 7.3). The aim is to make the categorization resulting from the data collection work operational (section 7.2.1) in order to propose a tool to help design these maps.

Among existing approaches, we have chosen to explore the possibilities offered by ontologies, because in addition to having an inference mechanism, this approach formalizes open-world modeling, which is more accurate to the non-exhaustive dimension of the information collected.

We therefore have chosen to model degrees of permanence and reliability using an ensemblistic approach, defining five individuals of a Degree class corresponding to the five semantic probabilities defined in section 7.2.2.1: *Null*, *Low*, *Moderate*, *High* and *Total*, then defining five degree classes as equivalent to the corresponding set of individuals: Total = {*Total*}, AtLeastHigh={*High*, *Total*}, AtLeastModerate={*Moderate*, *High*, *Total*}, TotheLowest={*Low*, *Moderate*, *High*, *Total*} and AtLeastNull={*Null*, *Low*, *Moderate*, *High*, *Total*}. The reason we have used [GLI 14] automatically deduces the overall hierarchy: Total $\subset$ AtLeastHigh $\subset$ AtLeastModerate $\subset$ TotheLowest $\subset$ AtLeastNull.

We then modeled sensory modalities by a main SensoryModality class, itself broken down into two AccessibleSensoryModality and NonAccessibleSensoryModality classes, each of which is equivalent to "SensoryModality & (*accessible to* some People)". Thus, objects instantiating the People class and *having access to* property (defined as the opposite of *accessible to*) defined by a *tactile*, *podotactile*, *visual*, etc., individual modality, will enable the logical reasoner to deduce which sensory modalities are accessible, and therefore should be considered next.

We then define the DetectableGeographicElement class equivalent to a GeographicElement with a *detectable* property defined by an AccessibleSensoryModality, then successively define the following classes:

1) SimpleLandmark: a DetectableGeographicElement with *permanent*, *distinctive* and *reliable* properties belonging to the Degree class.

2) CompoundLandmark: whose *composition* property is a DetectableGeographicElement and has *permanent*, *distinctive* and *reliable* properties belonging to the Degree class.

3) PrimaryLandmark: a DetectableGeographicElement, or whose *composition* property is a DetectableGeographicElement, and whose *permanent*, *distinctive* and *reliable* properties are all defined by an individual in the Total class.

4) SecondaryLandmark: a DetectableGeographicElement, or whose *composition* property is a DetectableGeographicElement, whose *permanent* and *distinctive* properties are defined by an individual of the

Total class, and whose *reliable* property is defined by an individual of the AtLeastModerate class.

5) InformationPoint: a DetectableGeographicElement, or whose *composition* property is a DetectableGeographicElement, whose *permanent* and *reliable* properties are defined by an individual of the Total class, and whose *distinctive* property is defined by an individual of the AtLeastModerate class.

The result is a model (Figure 7.3) that takes up the classification summarized in Figure 7.1, and enables the reasoner to deduce that a correctly informed geographic object is a simple landmark, or that a composition of geographic objects is a compound landmark, while distinguishing primary and secondary landmarks and points of information according to the classification that emerged from the collection (section 7.2.1). The ontology in owl format is available for free download and distributed under a GPLv3 licence[2].

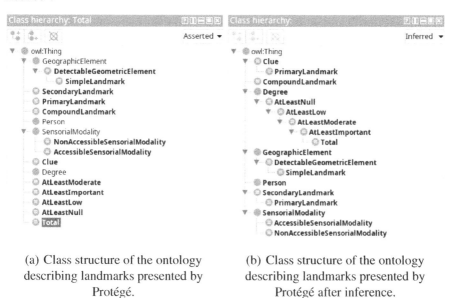

(a) Class structure of the ontology describing landmarks presented by Protégé.

(b) Class structure of the ontology describing landmarks presented by Protégé after inference.

Figure 7.3. *Landmark ontology for visually impaired people. For a color version of this figure, see www.iste.co.uk/pinet/geographic2.zip*

2 Available at: https://github.com/ACTIVmap/ontologie-reperes.

To illustrate how well the ontology works, we have added an individual `Person` with access to tactile and podotactile sensory cues, then added *Hedge*, *Gate* individuals and created a composite geographic object *HedgeGate* with total distinctive and permanence, but moderate reliability (it is necessary to follow the kerb to identify it with certainty). The logical reasoner deduces that this is a `CompoundLandmark` (Figure 7.4(a)) and a `SecondaryLandmark` (Figure 7.4(b)).

(a) HermiT's explanation of the `CompoundLandmark` inference: the logical reasoner infers from the ontology that the geographic object composed of a hedge and a gate is tactilely detectable, that this sensory modality is accessible to a blind person, and that it is therefore a compound landmark because it is distinctive, permanent, and moderately reliable, while being composed of at least one simple landmark.

(b) HermiT's explanation of the `SecondaryLandmark` inference: the logical reasoner deduces from the ontology that the geographic object composed of a hedge and a gate is detectable, and that being totally distinctive, totally permanent and moderately reliable, it is a secondary landmark.

Figure 7.4. *Examples of inferences obtained using the HermiT reasoner by populating the ontology with individuals representing a compound and secondary landmark. For a color version of this figure, see www.iste.co.uk/pinet/geographic2.zip*

7.2.3. *Model expressiveness*

In order to explore the daily practice of those with visual impairments, we conducted four interviews with the people concerned, asking them about their uses and habits during daily travel. In particular, we asked them to describe an itinerary as if they had done it for another visually impaired person. Table 7.1 gives a summary of these different descriptions: number of words in the description, length of the route described, number of clues or evidence we found in the description.

Person	Number of words	Length of route	Number of landmarks
L.	2,782	1.2 km then 3.7 km	45
J.-P.	784	3 km	10
N.	1,076	750 m	9
T.	736	500 m	23

Table 7.1. *Summary of the four route descriptions*

From these four descriptions, we can see a great diversity in terms of visual handicap (visually impaired, blind, congenital or not), a heterogeneity in ease of urban mobility, and also a greater or lesser degree of autonomy depending on the person.

Consequently, there is no marked correlation between the number of words, the length of the route or the number of landmarks evoked. Moreover, these landmarks are not always associated with the same scale of use. For example, the person who gave more than 20 landmarks for a 500-m route suggested a succession of very local elements ("I arrive at a place in front of the school where there are no more kerbs on the right, and there's a little gully that I follow"). The person describing a 3 km itinerary with only 10 landmarks has summarized long distances in a short sentence, leaving the recipient with less information ("there are about 10 streets to go through, some with traffic lights, others without; and then you'll feel like you're going under a bridge").

In the remainder of this section, we will discuss some typical examples of landmarks mentioned in these descriptions.

A bookseller's stall

In one of our surveys, when walking down a pedestrian street, a participant said: "[...] move along leaving a store on the left with a display of books in front of it, it's a bookseller...". This is a distinctive feature of this street, where it is the only stall present. It is only moderately permanent, because it depends on the bookshop's opening hours, and only moderately reliable, because if you walk on the other half of the road, you could miss this stall (Figure 7.5(a)).

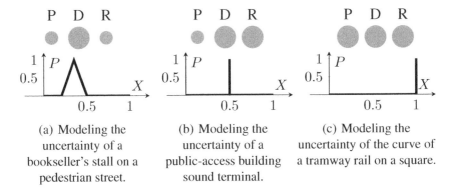

(a) Modeling the uncertainty of a bookseller's stall on a pedestrian street.

(b) Modeling the uncertainty of a public-access building sound terminal.

(c) Modeling the uncertainty of the curve of a tramway rail on a square.

Figure 7.5. *Classification and fuzzy number modeling the probability of detecting objects from itineraries collected during interviews with visually impaired people. For a color version of this figure, see www.iste.co.uk/pinet/geographic2.zip*

A sound terminal

In another survey, a participant commented: "with streets to cross, at some point you pass the FNAC and if you've activated the remote control, the FNAC has a terminal. So, once again, you know you're on the right track". In addition to traffic lights, it is becoming increasingly common in large cities for those with visual impairments to have sound terminals at their entrances, which can be activated with a dedicated remote control. The sound terminal generally works only when the public-access building is open, so this marker is moderately permanent, but is reliable because it can be triggered by a remote control from a distance of up to 10 m, and is distinctive because the audio message broadcast by the terminal gives the name of the sign (Figure 7.5(b)).

Tramway track curve

In a third survey, a participant said: "[...] here we're going to cross the tramway avenue, which is easy to spot because you can feel the tracks with your walking stick. You cross them, and you can walk along the tramway track. It bends a little to the right, so you can't go wrong in this relatively large square". The track of this tramway is permanent, it is reliable by following the orthogonal route described by the participant and the bend is distinctive of a precise location on the square. So here we have a primary reference point (Figure 7.5(c)).

7.3. Integration of landmarks in tactile and multimodal maps

As part of the ACTIVmap project[3], we are exploring the issue of representing urban space for the visually impaired by extending the experiments with tactile, tangible and sound devices proposed in the literature [DUC 15]. The density of information that can be represented on a tactile document is much less than that which can be represented on a drawn map [TOU 19a], which means that representation choices have to be made. By integrating text-based interactions into the map, we are considering a way of representing information that would have no place on the physical medium, either because the density would be too great, or because the uncertainty of its detection would be too great.

The literature and tools devoted to the generalization process offer a number of approaches [TOU 19b] which, among other things, enable us to decide on the presence of a geographic object on a map by integrating into the decision process the density of objects represented in its vicinity, as well as its class.

Drawing on this contextual decision-making process, we propose in this section to outline the contours of a generalization tool dedicated to maps intended for visually impaired people. The aim is to represent and share landmarks useful for urban mobility. We will build this proposal on the basis of fuzzy number modeling 7.2.2.1 and ontology classification 7.2.2.2 of these landmarks.

7.3.1. *Background map*

For several years now, we have been collecting 3D maps created for the visually impaired, for instance, as part of calls for contributions[4].

---

3 Available at: https://activmap.limos.fr.
4 Available at: https://compas.limos.fr/collectes/.

Various techniques are used to produce these maps, the most widespread today being thermal inflation, a technique which consists of printing the map on a special paper and placing it in an oven, where the black parts swell under the effect of heat. This type of printing is generally done on A4 sheets, more rarely A3, but never larger, for ease of reading [GEM 01]. As with maps for sighted people, generalization and stylization depend on scale. Thus, a map representing a neighborhood (Figure 7.6) will not show sidewalks or crosswalks, whereas a map at the scale of a square or crossroads will be much more precise, going so far as to show traffic islands, sidewalks and crosswalks, as on the map in Figure 7.7(a) from our collection, and created by a professional from the CRDV[5] in 2018.

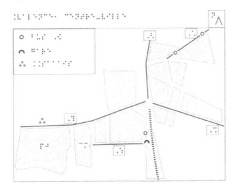

(a) Hand-produced map of downtown Valencia for thermal inflation (CTRCV 2016). This map is completed by an A4 sheet containing the legend and specifying the street names here indicated by two Braille characters.

(b) Hand-produced map of Besançon's historic center for high-contrast printing (CREESDEV 2018).

Figure 7.6. *Examples of city- or neighborhood-scale maps from our collection. For a color version of this figure, see www.iste.co.uk/pinet/geographic2.zip*

In this chapter, as in the ACTIVmap project as a whole, we have chosen to focus our attention on the scale of the crossroads, whose lack of available representations is a real obstacle to understanding urban space and the mobility of the most vulnerable visually impaired people.

5 Centre de Rééducation pour Déficients Visuels, available at: https://www.crdv.asso.fr/.

Available geographic databases rarely contain information describing pedestrian paths geometrically. There are a few OpenData databases published by local players, such as OpenData Paris[6], but no equivalent public data exist on a national, let alone global, scale. The most commonly explored method for automatically producing maps for visually impaired people [TOU 19a] is to exploit data from OpenStreetMap, which offers the advantage of excellent international coverage, and semantics refined year on year.

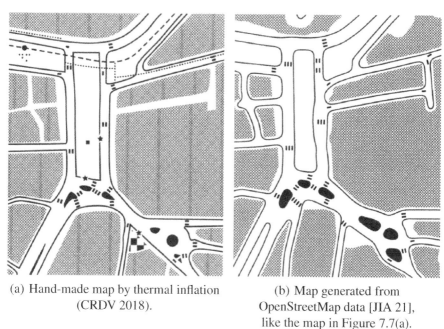

(a) Hand-made map by thermal inflation (CRDV 2018).

(b) Map generated from OpenStreetMap data [JIA 21], like the map in Figure 7.7(a).

Figure 7.7. *Example of a map showing a square with several complex intersections*

Figure 7.7 illustrates the various stages in map generation, starting with the transformation of linear streets into surfaces by applying a dilation or buffering operation (Figure 7.8(a)), then the generalization of buildings to simplify reading by touch (Figure 7.8(b)), by approximating city blocks by

6 "Les emprises au sol des trottoirs", extracted from the Paris street plan, available at: https://opendata.paris.fr/explore/dataset/plan-de-voirie-trottoirs-emprises/information/.

considering the complement of the linear streets (Figure 7.8(c)) and finally by generalizing the points describing crosswalks to obtain lines (Figure 7.8(d)).

(a) Extension of the street line to form   (b) Generalization of buildings to form
              street surfaces.   building blocks.

(c) Approximation of blocks from   (d) Generation of crosswalk lines
         street geometry.   from points.

Figure 7.8. *Steps in the production of a 3D map [JIA 21] from OpenStreetMap data. For a color version of this figure, see www.iste.co.uk/pinet/geographic2.zip*

7.3.2. *Integration of landmarks*

In this work, we would like to propose a map that is adapted to its readers, that is, satisfying both the needs and abilities of reading the map itself (tactile reading skills, ability to construct a mental map of a space) and the needs for information to be represented on the map. However, these two requirements can become contradictory, particularly when the density of information to be represented becomes too great. It is therefore essential to propose an approach that prioritizes the most significant and useful elements for orientation and mobility, while making the most of both representation modalities (tactile and audio). It should be noted that audio elements must be associated with tactile objects (such as characteristic pictograms) so that the user can identify and trigger them [DUC 15], for example, by means of a long press[7] or a double-tap[8].

– The essential geographical objects are the primary landmarks, which we propose to place on the map in an explicit and tactile manner, as they constitute, in the same way as the road elements presented in section 7.3.1, structuring elements of the described urban space. Represented in a punctual manner, whereas the other elements are linear, a separation gap can be used to distinguish two objects in relief by separating them with a gap[9] to make them legible with the fingers.

– Geographical objects which are distinctive, but not permanent or reliable, may be interesting to represent on the map if their description gives an idea of their permanence and reliability (e.g. a bookseller's stall cited in one of the interviews presented in section 7.2.3). In this case, we prefer to represent them by sound description, choosing to add them progressively to the map until tactile density is reached using the order given by the associated fuzzy number cluster (section 7.2.2.1).

– Finally, we propose to consider information points (nondistinctive elements), and to represent on the map those that can be used as confirmatory landmarks. Indeed, if a landmark is undistinctive because it is very present in its immediate vicinity (e.g. a paved surface, or a row of trees along a lane), but these elements are not found in other adjacent lanes, it is an interesting element to add to the description of the branch corresponding to the end junction [KAL 21b].

By way of illustration, we propose to use the information available in OpenStreetMap to enrich the background map shown in Figure 7.7(b).

– To the south of Place Salford, OSM data identify a platform with a bus shelter, corresponding to the stop for buses 3, 4 and 7[10] (Figure 7.9(a) ①). This urban equipment is permanent, distinctive as it is unique in this neighborhood and reliable as it occupies the entire width of the sidewalk (●●●). In the same way as the map produced by a CRDV professional (Figure 7.7(a)), we

---

7 FeelObject's Virtuoz device, available at: https://www.feelobject.fr/.

8 Tablet with embossed printed cover, Accessimap project, available at: https://www.irit.fr/accessimap/en/.

9 Also called comfort gap, the separation gap allows two 3D objects to be distinguished by separating them by a gap [GEM 01].

10 Available at: https://www.openstreetmap.org/way/939983548.

suggest positioning a pictogram whose distinctive shape (Figure 7.9(b) ⋆) will be included in the legend. This primary landmark can be augmented with audio information from OSM data, such as the numbers of the lines running to this stop.

– To the north of the Place Salford, OSM data show one of the exits from a high school[11] (Figure 7.9(a) ②). At peak school times, this is a very busy and noisy sidewalk, reliable and distinctive in this area, although not permanent (●●●). We therefore propose to add an audio description dedicated to this information, and identified on the tactile map by a pictogram dedicated to secondary landmarks (Figure 7.9(b) ●).

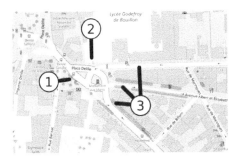 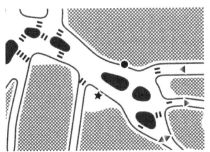

(a) Examples of primary landmarks (1), secondary landmarks (2), and location landmarks (3).

(b) Background map for tactile printing enhanced with symbols associated with the landmarks detected.

Figure 7.9. *Enhancement of a background map for tactile printing using the corresponding OSM data. For a color version of this figure, see www.iste.co.uk/pinet/geographic2.zip*

– To the southeast of Place Salford, three streets (Avenue Charras, Avenue Albert et Élisabeth and Avenue de Grande-Bretagne) lead off to the east or southeast (Figure 7.9(a) ③). Two of these are lined with trees on both sides of the lane, while the third has none. These rows of trees are mentioned in OpenStreetMap. Each tree is permanent, the reliability of detection is quite good (their locations occupy a large space on the narrow sidewalk), but each tree is undistinctive, due to the row structure (●·●). However, this information is distinctive of two of the branches, and therefore it can be used as

11 Available at: https://www.openstreetmap.org/node/4153877219.

a *confirmation marker*. It is therefore proposed to add to the description of each of these branches [KAL 21b] the corresponding precision (on the pictograms indicating the direction of traffic, Figure 7.9(b)):

- *The branch toward Saint-Joseph church, Avenue Charras, has two lanes of outbound traffic.* **This road is not lined with trees.**

- *The branch toward the SNCF train station, Avenue Albert et Élisabeth, has one outbound lane.* **This road is lined with trees.**

- *The branch toward Lycée Jeanne d'Arc, called Avenue de Grande-Bretagne, has three lanes: two outbound lanes and one inbound lane.* **This road is lined with trees.**

7.4. Integrating uncertainty into text descriptions

All of the text messages, whose voice synthesis is generated by double-tapping on the map's embossed elements, should enable the reader to perceive the different dimensions of uncertainty that they will encounter as they travel through the space described.

First, we propose to integrate the fuzzy probability of detecting landmarks in the structure of the spoken sentence (section 7.2.2.1). In a second step, we propose to consider the perceptive and usage capacities of the recipients of these maps by favoring the integration of fuzzy descriptions of distances and angles in the texts of the crossroads in which you are the main character [KAL 21a].

7.4.1. *Integrating the probability of detecting landmarks*

In section 7.3.2, we describe how to materialize the various landmarks on the map, using tactile pictograms specific to the feature, or pictograms indicating a more generic landmark.

In this second case, the textual description is essential, and must give the user enough information to measure the probability of detecting this landmark, both with permanence information, and with reliability information. As we have noted above, a moderately reliable landmark can be transformed into a conditional landmark if we can include location information in the description.

We therefore propose to construct the sentence by first indicating the uncertainty of permanence if it exists ("When [condition]"), then a formulation that includes the uncertainty of reliability if necessary ("you may encounter [...]"). Here, we have a few sentences that illustrate this construction:

– permanent, reliable landmark: "Paved garage exit";

– permanent and moderately reliable landmark: "You might come across a tree";

– a moderately permanent and reliable landmark: "When the FNAC store is open, you can trigger the audible beacon at its entrance";

– moderately permanent and moderately reliable landmark: "When the bookseller's stall is present, you may come across it", which could be made conditional by adding "When the bookseller's stall is present, you may come across it by walking down the left-hand wall" if you have an altitude measurement that identifies that the street has a slight incline.

7.4.2. *Integrating blurred distances and angles*

While the use of precise measurements (meters, degrees) in GPS descriptions is commonplace, we can reasonably question the relevance of this way of describing space when we know that the precision of a conventional GPS can very quickly deteriorate in urban environments. Also, visually impaired people have a capacity for angular discrimination and distance estimation that is very dependent on conditions and the environment [RAT 19].

The first descriptions of the crossroads of which you are the main character [KAL 21b] incorporated measurements suggested by users during our initial explorations: distances in meters, and angles expressed in hourly angles ("at 2 o'clock", "at 11 o'clock"), as is customary during exchanges between locomotion instructors and the visually impaired in learning situations.

However, when generating the text, we are unable to locate the listener precisely in space. If we want to describe the path to a crosswalk on the street perpendicular to the one we have just crossed, we need to consider the lateral and angular localization errors induced by the impossibility of following the crosswalk in a straight line.

On the other hand, simply indicating a clockwise angle does not take into account the possible orientation error when the person performs the indicated rotation. The literature tends to show that this rotation is often approximated and a slight rotation (around 45°) induces a greater approximation [AHM 18].

We therefore propose here to make the angles more flexible, so as not to include in the description a measurement that would be erroneous in a given situation. One possible approach is to divide the rotation space by labeling each section with an instruction [AHM 18]. For a frontal rotation, we propose a division into seven sections (Figure 7.10), allowing rotations to the right or left to benefit from three levels of finesse. While labeling angles close to 0°, 90° and 180° is "obvious", describing an intermediate angle seems less immediate. In the case of a single intermediate angle, the literature proposes the term "slightly" [AHM 18, GUE 18], but does not propose a term for a larger division. Based on the practices of a team of locomotion instructors asked about this issue, we have chosen to use the terms "slightly" and "a little more than slightly".

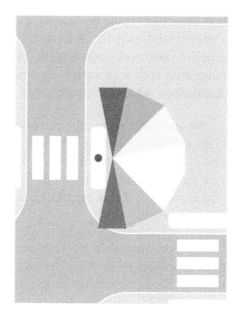

To the left

A little more than slightly to the left

Slightly to the left

In front

Slightly to the right

A little more than slightly to the right

To the right

Figure 7.10. *Proposed instructions associated with the seven sections of the forward rotation practiced by a team of locomotion instructors consulted on the issue. For a color version of this figure, see www.iste.co.uk/pinet/geographic2.zip*

Following Fazzi and Barlow [FAZ 17], distances will benefit from a similar approach, relying on divisions whose precision will be proportional to proximity: "a few steps away", "a few meters away", etc.

7.5. Conclusion and perspectives

In this chapter, we have presented a collection of the practices and needs of visually impaired people and the guidance and mobility professionals who work with them, and highlight the essential role that landmarks play in the construction of an urban journey. We have also identified one of the main challenges we face when describing them: the different modalities of uncertainty concerning them.

To model these landmarks and their uses, we proposed two tools: the use of a fuzzy number to describe the probability of finding a geographical object depending on its permanence and reliability, and ontology modeling to capture the diversity of landmark categories and purposes. We then showed how these tools could be used to select and then present useful landmarks on a multimodal map for the visually impaired. We proposed integrating an adaptive landmark positioning step into the map generation process, integrating both a geometric constraint, but also making the most of verbal descriptions, which are conducive to describing uncertainties.

We see these proposals as essential preliminary work for the design of maps incorporating these landmarks, and are now planning to use the results presented in this chapter to enrich the generative model of the crossroads that you are the main character of. This integration will enable us to test the reproducibility of this approach, and its relevance to the data available in OpenStreetMap.

The first maps thus materialized will provide an opportunity to evaluate these proposals by carrying out an evaluation with the visually impaired, on the one hand, presenting people who have proposed a route description (section 7.2.3) with maps derived from their descriptions, and then by setting up evaluations involving people who are not yet familiar with the mapped territories.

7.6. Acknowledgments

The authors would like to thank Bernard Oriola and Lachezar Dimitrov for the discussions that led to the questionnaire and the interviews with the people involved, and Manon Barret for regular exchanges on the practices of locomotion instructors. Special thanks also to Christophe Rey for the exchanges around ontologies that contributed to the modeling presented in this chapter. This work is funded by the Agence Nationale de la Recherche, ACTIVmap project (ANR-19-CE19-0005).

7.7. References

[AHM 18] AHMETOVIC D., OH U., MASCETTI S., et al., "Turn right: Analysis of rotation errors in turn-by-turn navigation for individuals with visual impairments", *Proceedings of the 20th International ACM SIGACCESS Conference on Computers and Accessibility*, ACM, Galway, pp. 333–339, 2018.

[BAL 12] BALTENNECK N., PORTALIER S., CHAPON P.-M., et al., "Parcourir la ville sans voir : effet de l'environnement urbain sur la perception et le ressenti des personnes aveugles lors d'un déplacement in situ", *L'Annee psychologique*, vol. 112, no. 3, pp. 403–433, 2012.

[DEV 19] DEVILLERS R., DESJARDIN E., DE RUNZ C. "Imperfection of geographic information: Concepts and terminologies", in BATTON-HUBERT M., DESJARDIN E., PINET F. (eds), *Geographic Data Imperfection 1: From Theory to Applications*, ISTE Ltd, London, and John Wiley & Sons, New York, 2019.

[DOW 77] DOWNS R.M., STEA D., *Maps in Minds: Reflections on Cognitive Mapping*, Harper Collins Publishers, New York, 1977.

[DUC 15] DUCASSE J., MACÉ M., JOUFFRAIS C., "From open geographical data to tangible maps: Improving the accessibility of maps for visually impaired people", *GeoVIS'15-ISPRS Geospatial Week (GeoVIS 2015)*, ISPRS, La Grande Motte, 517–523, 2015.

[FAZ 17] FAZZI D.L., BARLOW J.M., *Orientation and Mobility Techniques: A Guide for the Practitioner*, 2nd edition, American Printing House for the Blind, New York, 2017.

[GEM 01] GEM-EF, Guide de l'acheteur public de produits graphiques en relief à l'usage des personnes déficientes visuelles, Report, Observatoire de l'achat public, Ministère des finances, 2001.

[GLI 14] GLIMM B., HORROCKS I., MOTIK B., et al., "HermiT: An OWL 2 reasoner", *Journal of Automated Reasoning*, vol. 53, no. 3, pp. 245–269, 2014.

[GUE 18] GUERREIRO J., OHN-BAR E., AHMETOVIC D., et al., "How context and user behavior affect indoor navigation assistance for blind people", *Proceedings of the 15th International Web for All Conference*, ACM, Lyon, 2018.

[JIA 21] JIANG M.Y., CHRISTOPHE S., LOBO M.-J., et al., "Mapping road crossings for the visually impaired, a first experiment", *Journées de la Recherche IGN, Saint-Mandé (France)*, vol. 3, p. 127, available at: https://ica-abs.copernicus.org/articles/3/127/2021/, 2021.

[KAL 21a] KALSRON J., FAVREAU J.-M., TOUYA G., Le carrefour dont vous êtes le héros, Communications poster, Spatial Analysis and Geomatics (SAGEO), May 2021.

[KAL 21b] KALSRON J., FAVREAU J.-M., TOUYA G., "Le carrefour dont vous êtes le héros", *Journées de la Recherche IGN, Saint-Mandé (France)*, vol. 30, p. 19, 2021.

[LON 97] LONG R.G., HILL E., "Establishing and maintaining orientation for mobility", in BLASCH B.B., WIENER W.R., WELSH R.L. (eds), *Foundations of Orientation and Mobility*, vol. 1, AFB Press, New York, 1997.

[RAT 19] RATELLE A., *Manuel d'intervention en orientation et mobilité*, Presses de l'Université de Montréal, Montreal, 2019.

[STA 07] STANKIEWICZ B.J., KALIA A.A., "Acquistion of structural versus object landmark knowledge", *Journal of Experimental Psychology: Human Perception and Performance*, vol. 33, no. 2, p. 378, 2007.

[THI 97] THINUS-BLANC C., GAUNET F., "Representation of space in blind persons: Vision as a spatial sense?", *Psychological Bulletin*, vol. 121, no. 1, p. 20, 1997.

[TOU 19a] TOUYA G., CHRISTOPHE S., FAVREAU J.-M., et al., "Automatic derivation of on-demand tactile maps for visually impaired people: First experiments and research agenda", *International Journal of Cartography*, vol. 5, no. 1, pp. 67–91, 2019.

[TOU 19b] TOUYA G., LOKHAT I., DUCHÊNE C., "CartAGen: An open source research platform for map generalization", *International Cartographic Conference 2019*, vol. 2, pp. 1–9, 2019.

List of Authors

Mireille BATTON-HUBERT
École des Mines de Saint-Étienne
Institut Henri Fayol
UMR LIMOS
Saint-Étienne
France

Delphine BLANKE
LMA
Avignon
France

Guilhem BOULAY
UMR ESPACE
Avignon
France

Mattia BUNEL
LASTIG
Université Gustave Eiffel
IGN-ENSG
Saint-Mandé
France

Laure CASANOVA ENAULT
UMR ESPACE
Avignon
France

Mathieu COULON
UMR ESPACE
Aix-en-Provence
France

Paule-Annick DAVOINE
PACTE
Université Grenoble Alpes
France

Lisa DENIS
UCA
Aubière
France

Eric DESJARDIN
CReSTIC
Université de Reims
Champagne-Ardenne
France

Cécile DUCHÊNE
LASTIG
Université Gustave Eiffel
IGN-ENSG
Champs-sur-Marne
France

Jean-Marie FAVREAU
UCA
Aubière
France

Jean-Michel FOLLIN
GeF
HESAM Université – CNAM
Le Mans
France

Marie FOURNIER
GeF
HESAM Université – CNAM
Le Mans
France

Jean-François GIRRES
Université Paul-Valéry III
Montpellier
France

Didier JOSSELIN
UMR ESPACE
Avignon
France

Jérémy KALSRON
UCA
Aubière
France

Florence LE BER
ICube
Université de Strasbourg
France

Pierre LE BRUN
UMR ESPACE
Avignon
France

Aurélie LEBORGNE
ICube
Université de Strasbourg
France

Thibault LECOURT
UMR ESPACE
Avignon
France

Stella MARC-ZWECKER
Icube
Université de Strasbourg
France

André MIRALLES
UMR TETIS
INRAE
Montpellier
France

Ana-Maria OLTEANU-RAIMOND
LASTIG
Université Gustave Eiffel
IGN-ENSG
Saint-Mandé
France

Antoine PERIS
UMR ESPACE
Avignon
France

François PINET
TSCF
INRAE
Clermont-Ferrand
France

Ezriel STEINBERG
ICube
Université de Strasbourg
France

Nathalie THOMMERET
GeF
HESAM Université – CNAM
Le Mans
France

Marlène VILLANOVA
LIG
Université Grenoble Alpes
France

Matthieu VIRY
LIG
Université Grenoble Alpes
France

Index

Other titles from

in

Information Systems, Web and Pervasive Computing

2023

POMEROL Jean-Charles
Action in Uncertainty: Expertise, Decision and Crisis Management

REVEST Valérie, LIOTARD Isabelle
Digital Transformation and Public Policies: Current Issues

2022

ACCART Jean-Philippe
Library Transformation Strategies

BOADA Martí, LAZARO Antonio, GIRBAU David, VILLARINO Ramón
Battery-less NFC Sensors for the Internet of Things

BRÉZILLON Patrick, TURNER Roy M.
Modeling and Use of Context in Action

CHAMOUX Jean-Pierre
The Digital Era 3: Customs and Practices

KARAM Elie
General Contractor Business Model for Smart Cities: Fundamentals and Techniques

2021

BEN REBAH Hassen, BOUKTHIR Hafedh, CHÉDEBOIS Antoine
Website Design and Development with HTML5 and CSS3

EL ASSAD Safwan, BARBA Dominique
Digital Communications 1: Fundamentals and Techniques
Digital Communications 2: Directed and Practical Work

GAUDIN Thierry, MAUREL Marie-Christine, POMEROL Jean-Charles
Chance, Calculation and Life

LAURENT Sébastien-Yves
Conflicts, Crimes and Regulations in Cyberspace
(Cybersecurity Set – Volume 2)

LE DEUFF Olivier
Hyperdocumentation (Intellectual Technologies Set – Volume 9)

PÉLISSIER Maud
Cultural Commons in the Digital Ecosystem
(Intellectual Technologies Set – Volume 8)

2020

CLIQUET Gérard, with the collaboration of BARAY Jérôme
Location-Based Marketing: Geomarketing and Geolocation

DE FRÉMINVILLE Marie
Cybersecurity and Decision Makers: Data Security and Digital Trust

GEORGE Éric
Digitalization of Society and Socio-political Issues 2: Digital, Information and Research

HELALI Saida
Systems and Network Infrastructure Integration

LOISEAU Hugo, VENTRE Daniel, ADEN Hartmut
Cybersecurity in Humanities and Social Sciences: A Research Methods Approach (Cybersecurity Set – Volume 1)

GHLALA Riadh
Analytic SQL in SQL Server 2014/2016

JANIER Mathilde, SAINT-DIZIER Patrick
Argument Mining: Linguistic Foundations

SOURIS Marc
Epidemiology and Geography: Principles, Methods and Tools of Spatial Analysis

TOUNSI Wiem
Cyber-Vigilance and Digital Trust: Cyber Security in the Era of Cloud Computing and IoT

2018

ARDUIN Pierre-Emmanuel
Insider Threats
(Advances in Information Systems Set – Volume 10)

CARMÈS Maryse
Digital Organizations Manufacturing: Scripts, Performativity and Semiopolitics
(Intellectual Technologies Set – Volume 5)

CARRÉ Dominique, VIDAL Geneviève
Hyperconnectivity: Economical, Social and Environmental Challenges
(Computing and Connected Society Set – Volume 3)

CHAMOUX Jean-Pierre
The Digital Era 1: Big Data Stakes

DOUAY Nicolas
Urban Planning in the Digital Age
(Intellectual Technologies Set – Volume 6)

FABRE Renaud, BENSOUSSAN Alain
The Digital Factory for Knowledge: Production and Validation of Scientific Results

GAUDIN Thierry, LACROIX Dominique, MAUREL Marie-Christine, POMEROL Jean-Charles
Life Sciences, Information Sciences

GAYARD Laurent
Darknet: Geopolitics and Uses
(Computing and Connected Society Set – Volume 2)

IAFRATE Fernando
Artificial Intelligence and Big Data: The Birth of a New Intelligence
(Advances in Information Systems Set – Volume 8)

LE DEUFF Olivier
Digital Humanities: History and Development
(Intellectual Technologies Set – Volume 4)

MANDRAN Nadine
Traceable Human Experiment Design Research: Theoretical Model and Practical Guide
(Advances in Information Systems Set – Volume 9)

PIVERT Olivier
NoSQL Data Models: Trends and Challenges

ROCHET Claude
Smart Cities: Reality or Fiction

SALEH Imad, AMMI, Mehdi, SZONIECKY Samuel
Challenges of the Internet of Things: Technology, Use, Ethics
(Digital Tools and Uses Set – Volume 7)

SAUVAGNARGUES Sophie
Decision-making in Crisis Situations: Research and Innovation for Optimal Training

SEDKAOUI Soraya
Data Analytics and Big Data

SZONIECKY Samuel
Ecosystems Knowledge: Modeling and Analysis Method for Information and Communication
(Digital Tools and Uses Set – Volume 6)

2017

BOUHAÏ Nasreddine, SALEH Imad
Internet of Things: Evolutions and Innovations
(Digital Tools and Uses Set – Volume 4)

DUONG Véronique
Baidu SEO: Challenges and Intricacies of Marketing in China

LESAS Anne-Marie, MIRANDA Serge
The Art and Science of NFC Programming
(Intellectual Technologies Set – Volume 3)

LIEM André
Prospective Ergonomics
(Human-Machine Interaction Set – Volume 4)

MARSAULT Xavier
Eco-generative Design for Early Stages of Architecture
(Architecture and Computer Science Set – Volume 1)

REYES-GARCIA Everardo
The Image-Interface: Graphical Supports for Visual Information
(Digital Tools and Uses Set – Volume 3)

REYES-GARCIA Everardo, BOUHAÏ Nasreddine
Designing Interactive Hypermedia Systems
(Digital Tools and Uses Set – Volume 2)

SAÏD Karim, BAHRI KORBI Fadia
Asymmetric Alliances and Information Systems:Issues and Prospects
(Advances in Information Systems Set – Volume 7)

SZONIECKY Samuel, BOUHAÏ Nasreddine
Collective Intelligence and Digital Archives: Towards Knowledge Ecosystems
(Digital Tools and Uses Set – Volume 1)

2016

BEN CHOUIKHA Mona
Organizational Design for Knowledge Management

BERTOLO David
Interactions on Digital Tablets in the Context of 3D Geometry Learning
(Human-Machine Interaction Set – Volume 2)

BOUVARD Patricia, SUZANNE Hervé
Collective Intelligence Development in Business

EL FALLAH SEGHROUCHNI Amal, ISHIKAWA Fuyuki, HÉRAULT Laurent, TOKUDA Hideyuki
Enablers for Smart Cities

FABRE Renaud, in collaboration with MESSERSCHMIDT-MARIET Quentin, HOLVOET Margot
New Challenges for Knowledge

GAUDIELLO Ilaria, ZIBETTI Elisabetta
Learning Robotics, with Robotics, by Robotics
(Human-Machine Interaction Set – Volume 3)

HENROTIN Joseph
The Art of War in the Network Age
(Intellectual Technologies Set – Volume 1)

KITAJIMA Munéo
Memory and Action Selection in Human–Machine Interaction
(Human–Machine Interaction Set – Volume 1)

LAGRAÑA Fernando
E-mail and Behavioral Changes: Uses and Misuses of Electronic Communications

LEIGNEL Jean-Louis, UNGARO Thierry, STAAR Adrien
Digital Transformation
(Advances in Information Systems Set – Volume 6)

NOYER Jean-Max
Transformation of Collective Intelligences
(Intellectual Technologies Set – Volume 2)

VENTRE Daniel
Information Warfare – 2nd edition

VITALIS André
The Uncertain Digital Revolution
(Computing and Connected Society Set – Volume 1)

2015

ARDUIN Pierre-Emmanuel, GRUNDSTEIN Michel, ROSENTHAL-SABROUX Camille
Information and Knowledge System
(Advances in Information Systems Set – Volume 2)

BÉRANGER Jérôme
Medical Information Systems Ethics

BRONNER Gérald
Belief and Misbelief Asymmetry on the Internet

IAFRATE Fernando
From Big Data to Smart Data
(Advances in Information Systems Set – Volume 1)

KRICHEN Saoussen, BEN JOUIDA Sihem
Supply Chain Management and its Applications in Computer Science

NEGRE Elsa
Information and Recommender Systems
(Advances in Information Systems Set – Volume 4)

POMEROL Jean-Charles, EPELBOIN Yves, THOURY Claire
MOOCs

2012

BUCHER Bénédicte, LE BER Florence
Innovative Software Development in GIS

GAUSSIER Eric, YVON François
Textual Information Access

STOCKINGER Peter
Audiovisual Archives: Digital Text and Discourse Analysis

VENTRE Daniel
Cyber Conflict

2011

BANOS Arnaud, THÉVENIN Thomas
Geographical Information and Urban Transport Systems

DAUPHINÉ André
Fractal Geography

LEMBERGER Pirmin, MOREL Mederic
Managing Complexity of Information Systems

STOCKINGER Peter
Introduction to Audiovisual Archives

STOCKINGER Peter
Digital Audiovisual Archives

VENTRE Daniel
Cyberwar and Information Warfare

2010

BONNET Pierre
Enterprise Data Governance

BRUNET Roger
Sustainable Geography

KANEVSKI Michael
Advanced Mapping of Environmental Data

MANOUVRIER Bernard, LAURENT Ménard
Application Integration: EAI, B2B, BPM and SOA

PAPY Fabrice
Digital Libraries

2007

DOBESCH Hartwig, DUMOLARD Pierre, DYRAS Izabela
Spatial Interpolation for Climate Data

SANDERS Lena
Models in Spatial Analysis

2006

CLIQUET Gérard
Geomarketing

CORNIOU Jean-Pierre
Looking Back and Going Forward in IT

DEVILLERS Rodolphe, JEANSOULIN Robert
Fundamentals of Spatial Data Quality

Printed and bound by CPI Group (UK) Ltd, Croydon, CR0 4YY

27/10/2024

14580735-0001